STUDENT'S TRANSCRIPT OF

SPEED BUILDING

FOR COLLEGES

DIAMOND JUBILEE SERIES

STUDENT'S TRANSCRIPT OF

SPEED BUILDING
FOR COLLEGES
DIAMOND JUBILEE SERIES

JOHN R. GREGG

CLYDE I. BLANCHARD
ADMINISTRATIVE MANAGEMENT CONSULTANT
FORMERLY PROFESSOR OF BUSINESS EDUCATION
UNIVERSITY OF TULSA

WOODROW W. BALDWIN
DIRECTOR, SCHOOL OF BUSINESS ADMINISTRATION
SIMMONS COLLEGE

ESTELLE POPHAM
FORMERLY CHAIRMAN, DEPARTMENT OF BUSINESS EDUCATION
HUNTER COLLEGE

GREGG DIVISION   McGRAW-HILL BOOK COMPANY
NEW YORK ST. LOUIS DALLAS SAN FRANCISCO TORONTO LONDON SYDNEY

PUT YOUR TRANSCRIPT TO WORK FOR YOU

The *Student's Transcript* contains the transcript to the shorthand material in the Speed Building Practices, Transcription Speed Builders, Sustained Speed Builders, and Transcription Checkpoints and Pacers of *Gregg Speed Building for Colleges, Diamond Jubilee Series.* The number preceding each exercise corresponds to the shorthand exercise number in the text. This transcript serves three desirable purposes:

1 The student can quickly look up the word or phrase represented by any outline about which he is in doubt. The immediate reinforcement helps the student to cover more exercises more quickly and with a minimum of discouragement.

2 The student's attention is called to all the nonshorthand stumbling blocks, such as spelling, punctuation, capitalization, and number usage, helping him to eliminate all such errors from his transcripts.

3 Because the key material is counted, the student is able to obtain extra dictation practice outside the class.

By using the Conversion Table facing page 1, the student may ask friends to dictate the material in this transcript, which has been counted in groups of 20 standard words, at speeds ranging from 40 to 160 words a minute.

THE PUBLISHERS

UNIT 1▶   Lessons 1-5

CONVERSION TABLE FOR DICTATION SPEEDS
(Material Counted in Groups of 20 Standard Words)

\					WORDS PER MINUTE							
40	50	60	70	80	90	100	110	120	130	140	150	160
					TIME INTERVALS IN SECONDS							
30	24	20	17	15	13	12	11	10	9	8	8	7
60	48	40	34	30	26	24	22	20	18	17	16	15
30	12	60	51	45	40	36	33	30	27	25	24	22
60	36	20	08	60	53	48	44	40	37	34	32	30
	60	40	25	15	06	60	55	50	46	42	40	37
		60	42	30	20	12	06	60	55	51	48	45
			60	45	33	24	17	10	04	60	56	52
				60	47	36	28	20	14	08	04	60
					60	48	39	30	23	17	12	07
						60	50	40	32	25	20	15
							60	50	41	34	28	22
								60	51	42	36	30
									60	51	44	37
										60	52	45
											60	52
												60

Example: To use this chart in dictating material at 70 words a minute, follow this procedure: Locate the "70" column under the "Words per Minute" heading. In the same column, the first figure below the "Time Intervals in Seconds" heading is 17. Therefore, to dictate at 70 words a minute, dictate each group of 20 standard words in 17 seconds. The figures below 17 indicate the point on the watch where the second hand should be at the end of each additional group of 20 words of dictation. These time indications have been carried through the first two minutes.

Unit 1

LESSON 1

1▶ Dear Mr. Jones: Are you having a difficult time in moving your merchandise between states during the shipping[1] strike? Several manufacturers were caught unprepared when railroad and trucking services were stopped this week.[2] According to this morning's newspaper, the strike is likely to continue for several weeks.

I suggest that some[3] of those who have experienced the same problems meet to discuss the situation. What day would suit you best?[4] Do you prefer a morning or an afternoon meeting? We could use my club on Madison Street for the meeting[5] if that is satisfactory. Which manufacturers should we invite?

Once we have had an opportunity[6] to decide upon a course of action, we should be able to take immediate steps to solve the problem.[7] When I have your answer to this letter, I shall send a notice about the meeting to those who are to be[8] invited. Sincerely yours, (164)

2▶ Gentlemen: Yesterday I learned that I had won $40 worth of merchandise in your newspaper contest.[1] I have never won anything before, and I am delighted! I should like to thank you for giving me the[2] opportunity to take part in this competition.

Since the quantity of goods is small and I am away on[3] a short vacation, I should like to request that you hold the merchandise until I return and can select what[4] I want.

Please use the enclosed envelope to let me know whether this arrangement is satisfactory. Cordially[5] yours, (101)

3▶ Dear Mrs. Green: Yesterday I received a letter from Mr. James Browning telling me that I am to share[1] in an estate owned by my late brother. This is a very big surprise to me, for he had difficulty with[2] the family ten years ago and left the city. We have not heard from him directly during these years, although[3] we were told that he had gone to Denver, where he became a merchant.

I must have someone to represent me in[4] the settlement of this estate. Because of your particular knowledge of Colorado law, I think that you[5] are the right person. Would you represent me?

Please send me your answer as soon as possible so that I can make[6] my plans. If you would like to see me in person, I can catch a plane to Denver next Tuesday morning. Yours very[7] truly, (141)

4▶ Dear Mr. Wilson: You have

1

won the admiration of the public during your campaign, and I am glad to commend[1] you on your election.

I have never taken a particularly active part in politics, but I[2] have followed your progress with great interest. Throughout the several months when you made so many appearances[3] that were reported in the newspapers and in other publications, you were a model upon which other[4] men seeking public office could well fashion their campaigns.

Best wishes to you in your new office. I am sure that[5] you will serve the public well. Sincerely yours, (108)

5▸ Dear Mr. Hastings: I have read a great deal in the local newspaper about the crime situation throughout[1] the city, and I am taking this opportunity to express my concern over the problem.

I should like[2] to offer three suggestions, which I believe must be considered if we are to improve the situation:

1.[3] We must increase the number of policemen who are assigned to residential streets. You are aware that a large[4] number of crimes have been committed in these areas in the past several weeks.

2. We must provide more[5] protection at night, not only in the main part of the city but in the outlying areas as well.

3. We[6] must continue to improve our street lighting throughout the city. In some areas this situation is very[7] serious.

I do hope that something will be done about this situation, and I know that a large number[8] of people in this city feel the same way about it. Cordially yours, (173)

6▸ Dear Mr. Simpson: Once you have read our publication, Business World, we think that you will feel that you can never[1] be without it.

We should like to send Business World to you at the reduced rate of $7.50[2] during the next six weeks, for we think you will become a regular subscriber by the time you have read it that[3] long. Several key businessmen are being offered this special rate, which is a reduction of 30 percent[4] on the regular rate.

I am sending this week's issue to you. I hope that you will read it carefully. Then use[5] the self-addressed envelope to send us your order. Very sincerely yours, (114)

LESSON 2

7▸ Dear Mrs. Stevens: This letter acknowledges receipt of your correspondence with our representative in[1] the Memphis office, Mr. Frank White.

I appreciate your sending me this material, Mrs. Stevens, because[2] knowing the general background of the problem will help me to forestall repetition of your experience.[3] I cannot understand Mr. White's attitude in this matter; he has always been one of the finest representatives[4] the company has had in

2

that area.

I am planning a trip to Memphis within the coming[5] week, and I hope to see you and discuss the matter further with you. Of course, I shall see Mr. White while I am[6] there, too. In the meantime, if you can give me any additional information, I shall be pleased to receive[7] it.

Thank you for your help. Sincerely yours, (147)

8▶ Dear Mr. Harrison: I am pleased to answer your questions concerning my impressions of the Ford Manufacturing[1] Company.

About a year ago I accompanied our correspondent when he attended the annual[2] meeting of the shareholders of the Ford Manufacturing Company. I also assisted him[3] in preparing a report on the meeting, which was later printed in the business news section of the Toledo[4] Times.

This is a forward-looking company in every respect. It is one of the best-managed companies[5] that I have seen, and its record of profits is excellent. As you know, they have taken on several new[6] lines this year; therefore, I see a big growth picture for the next several years. My feeling is that an investment[7] in Ford would be a very sound one. Sincerely yours, (150)

9▶ Gentlemen: We should like to tell you about our experience in advertising in the Daily Herald. Although[1] advertisements of books characteristically have greater pulling power in the morning paper, we[2] have found that just the opposite is true in our latest advertisements on our new business handbook series. The[3] Wednesday edition of the Herald pulled the biggest response we have had to date — nearly twice as much as was received[4] from the leading morning newspaper, which has a much larger circulation.

The accompanying report[5] shows you the breakdown of responses by area. Isn't it surprising that so many responses came from[6] people who live more than 500 miles away? This speaks well for your wide circulation.

You may be sure that we[7] are more than satisfied with our results in the Daily Herald, and we expect to use your newspaper regularly[8] from now on. You may feel free to circularize this letter in any way you see fit. Yours very truly,[9] (180)

10▶ Dear Mr. Barry: Three weeks ago I placed an order for 500 manila correspondence folders, and[1] I accompanied the order with my check for $25. My order was never acknowledged, nor have[2] I received any word from you as to when I may expect to receive the folders. Generally, when I order[3] office supplies from your company, I can expect prompt and efficient service. This is why I am unable[4] to explain this particular delay.

If you are not able to ship these folders by April 15, please[5] cancel my order, for I shall have to obtain the folders elsewhere. We are already several weeks behind[6] in our filing reorganization because we have not had the necessary supplies. Yours very truly,[7] (140)

11▶ Dear Miss Phillips: It was a pleasure to read in last night's Los Angeles Leader of your election to the office[1] of president of the Business Women's Guild. I know this honor is an acknowledgment of your dedicated[2] service to the business community, and I think your fellow members showed excellent judgment in choosing[3] you.

Please know that everyone here at the Chamber of Commerce stands behind you and your organization in[4] all its activities. I hope that you will let us know how we can make your job easier. We forecast a great[5] year ahead for the Business Women's Guild under your leadership. Cordially yours, (114)

12▶ Dear Mr. Miller: Thank you for the businesslike way in which you handled the advertising for our big fund-raising[1] drive. Characteristically, you demonstrated your public spirit and your concern for the disadvantaged[2] by supporting us so effectively throughout the campaign. Not only did you give newspaper space generously,[3] but you also personally helped us to build large lists of prospective donors.

When we checked the pledge[4] envelopes yesterday, we discovered that the average pledge was $10 bigger than in any previous[5] campaign. We appreciate your help immensely. Sincerely yours, (112)

13▶ Gentlemen: You are a very important customer of ours, and we are wondering why you have not reordered[1] any of our Princess Lola handbags. Many stores in nearby cities have found these handbags are among their[2] best sellers during the Christmas season because they make ideal gifts.

The most popular features of the Princess[3] Lola are its smart shape, the handy new fastener, the secret enclosure for hiding big bills, and the[4] extraordinary wearing qualities. It is truly a versatile handbag that complements any outfit, whether[5] the owner uses it for business or social occasions.

May we suggest that you order an additional[6] quantity of ten dozen of the Princess Lola handbags. As a goodwill gesture, we will participate[7] with you in your promotion by preparing your newspaper advertising layouts and sharing the cost of the[8] advertisements. Although we do not ordinarily make offers of this kind, we are so convinced that you will benefit[9] greatly from pushing these handbags that we are willing to depart from our usual merchandising[10] procedures so that you may take advantage of the growing popularity of the Princess Lola handbag. Very[11] truly yours, (222)

14▶ Dear Professor Johnson: We are greatly impressed with your outline for the revision of our handbook in business[1] correspondence. The objectives are

4

clearly stated, and the organization is logical. By departing[2] from the ordinary format, you have overcome most of the objections to the present edition.

We suggest[3] that you increase the number of examples of correspondence characteristic of big and small business:[4] letters of acknowledgment, letters requesting adjustment, letters promoting goodwill, letters concerning[5] advertising and sales, and letters about credit and collections. Also, have you thought about the advantages[6] of adding an appendix so that the user can find reference material handily?

We foresee no[7] difficulty in publishing this handbook next year if you can work on it immediately. Ordinarily[8] we would obtain an opinion from users of our present handbook about possible changes in the book.[9] However, this time we shall bypass this step.

Please let us know when you plan to begin the handbook and the tentative[10] date of completion. Cordially yours, (207)

15▸ Dear Miss Hanson: I am glad to write in behalf of Mr. Ray Fields, who has applied for a government position.[1] Mr. Fields was in our organization for several years, during which time he held an important[2] position as general clerk. He was an ideal employee: we liked him and we liked his work. He was good-natured,[3] well organized, and efficient.

Mr. Fields' departure from our company was a great disappointment to[4] us, and we have missed him. In my opinion, he will be an asset to any organization. I recommend[5] him highly. Sincerely yours, (106)

16▸ Gentlemen: Your frank opinions about the present edition of our manufacturer's handbook, which we sent[1] you for review several weeks ago, have been very helpful. It is only through such suggestions as yours that[2] we can continue to improve this handbook and make it the important reference source it was designed to be.[3]

Your suggestions for reorganizing the section on quality control are particularly good, and we[4] have already passed them along to our editors for their guidance in preparing the next edition. I[5] appreciated also your comments on the layout of a parts department and the handling of employees' overtime.[6] All these suggestions are gratefully acknowledged, and I think you will see many of your ideas reflected[7] in the new third edition, which is to be published next May. Cordially yours, (155)

17▸ Dear Mrs. Smith: Although we have sent you several reminders, including two letters, we have not heard from you[1] concerning your overdue bill of $76.85. When the first reminders were sent, it[2] was my opinion that you had simply overlooked the bill and that you would pay it promptly. Such however, was[3] not the case, because you have made no overture toward paying your bill nor have you given us the courtesy of[4] an explanation.

If you would write or telephone me, I should be glad to arrange some plan whereby you could take[5] care of your account in convenient monthly payments. If I don't hear from you, however, I shall be forced to try[6] other means of collecting the amount due. I expect an answer to this letter within five days. Yours very[7] truly, (141)

LESSON 4

18▶ Dear Mr. Williams: We recently established a West Coast division of our magazine, Modern Home, and are[1] seeking an advertising agency to represent us in that area. The circulation in the western[2] states has grown to over 16,000 during the past two years, and we feel that manufacturers in that[3] area will want to reach this important market through our publication.

Modern Home, the successor to Today's[4] Builder, is a magazine for homeowners who take pride in their homes and gardens. It contains articles of[5] unusual interest on subjects ranging from how to build a bird feeder to how to decorate one's home[6] for Thanksgiving. The total circulation is 150,000, and it is growing at a very[7] satisfactory rate year by year. Although the magazine is obtainable at the present time only by[8] subscription, it is probable that we shall have it on newsstands within the next year or two.

You have successfully[9] represented a number of other publishers on the West Coast for many years and are recognized as[10] an authority in advertising layout and design. Would you be interested in discussing a contract[11] with us for handling our advertising in that area? Our managing editor, Mr. Clark Winters,[12] will be in Spokane on March 8, where he is to speak before the Pine Dealers Association. Would it be possible[13] for you to see him during his visit and discuss this matter further?

I shall be anxious to hear from[14] you. Cordially yours, (283)

19▶ Gentlemen: Are you satisfied with the envelopes you are now using for your advertising circulars? Our[1] new Time-Saver envelope will save you time and money, regardless of the type you are presently using and[2] regardless of what you are paying for it.

The Time-Saver comes in a wide variety of colors and sizes.[3] On orders of 100,000 or more, we will print your company symbol without additional cost.[4]

Our representative will be in Chicago on August 12. May he pay you a short visit to speak to you[5] about our line of envelopes? I believe you will find it worth your time to see him. Yours very sincerely,[6] (120)

20▶ Dear Mrs. Kane: I want to tell you how much I appreciate your suggestions for improving our public[1] relations through better customer service. Your ideas are very progressive, and they are sound in every[2] way.

I am sure you realize that one of the problems of bigness in any organization is the loss[3] of personal contact with regular customers. Although we realize that better merchandise and better[4] service have been responsible for our growth, we must not lose sight of the fact that bigness does not give any[5] organization the right to disregard the interests of the buying public.

You may be sure that we are thankful[6] for good customers like you, and we shall continue to serve you in the best possible manner. I hope that[7] you will write me whenever you have additional suggestions. Very cordially yours, (156)

21▶ Dear Mr. Parks: You have been recommended to us as an outstanding authority on the new regulations[1] concerning corporation taxes. The Accountants Society of New York is seeking a speaker for[2] its June 15 meeting, which will be devoted to this subject. Would your busy schedule permit you to be[3] with us on this date?

Our meeting begins with dinner at six-thirty, followed by the program at eight o'clock. We[4] would expect you to speak for about forty minutes, after which there would be general discussion of your[5] presentation by the members.

I am permitted to offer you a fee of $50, plus your travel and[6] hotel expenses. Please let me know whether you can participate in this program. If so, I will then send you[7] complete details. If you wish to have a hotel reservation, I shall be glad to make it for you. Cordially[8] yours, (161)

22▶ Dear Mr. Barnes: I am pleased to answer your questions concerning the statement of your December purchases.[1]

According to our records, there was a balance of $16.48 outstanding for purchases made[2] in November. This amount was included through error as a part of your December 14 invoice. It should[3] have been listed as a separate item.

The December 19 invoice is unquestionably in error,[4] because the five Atlas Tires you were charged for were not delivered. We are issuing a credit memorandum[5] of $72 for this amount. The total of the statement should now be $265.28,[6] which I hope you will find to be in agreement with your own records.

It is a pleasure to[7] do business with you. Cordially yours, (147)

LESSON 5

23▶ Dear Mr. Marks: We have received the timer that you returned to us and your request to repair it without cost[1] because you feel that the workmanship on it does not meet satisfactory standards.

I wish it were possible[2] to repair this timer for you without charge, but unfortunately the guarantee on it expired over a[3] year ago. As you know, the timers we manufacture are very low in cost; and we believe they represent[4] more value for the money than anything comparable on the market. At the same time, the fact that they are[5] priced well below the average prevents our guaranteeing them for more than a year.

I should like to suggest two[6] possible courses of action, either of which will be satisfactory to us. We will repair the old timer[7] for the special price of $4, or we will send you a new timer at a reduction of $3[8] from the regular price.

Please let us have your decision as soon as possible, Mr. Marks. In the meantime, we[9] shall keep the old timer until we hear from you. Sincerely yours, (192)

24▶ Dear Miss Knox: We should like very much to have you as our guest at the next regular meeting of the Chicago[1] Advertising Women's Club on May 16.

You may remember that at our May program each year the annual[2] advertising awards are presented to the young women who achieved distinction in advertising during[3] the preceding year. You have been chosen to make these presentations. Following the presentation of the awards,[4] we should like to have you speak to the group on the contribution of advertising to business and the role[5] of women in this important field.

Among our guests at this meeting will be a group of young women from Overton[6] College. They are very much interested in advertising as a field of work, and I know that they would[7] be pleased to hear about some of your experiences in advertising and especially about your impressions[8] of the World Advertising Council meeting that you attended in Paris earlier this year.

Can you make[9] arrangements to attend this meeting and participate as I have suggested? We should be very glad to have[10] you. We will take care of your expenses, including travel and hotel accommodations. Of course, you will be[11] our guest at dinner. Incidentally, the meeting is to be held in the Rooftop Lounge of the Republic Hotel.[12]

I shall be anxious to have your reply. In the meantime, I am enclosing a circular that our chapter[13] has just issued — "Women in Advertising." Perhaps you will find it interesting. If you wish to have additional[14] copies, just let me know. Very sincerely yours, (290)

25▶ Dear Dean Mason: This year our Marketing Department is undertaking a study of world markets in the[1] appliance industry. We are seeking information on consumer preferences, buying motives, and package[2] design; and we have mailed thousands of questionnaires to dealers all over the world.

The questionnaires are now[3] coming in, and we shall need about six additional people to assist us in analyzing them and preparing[4] our final report. Do you have several undergraduates available whom you could recommend to[5] us for the summer? We would need them from about June 10 to August 15. Although no special skills are required,[6] we should like these people to be able to type and use an adding machine. The salary will be $70[7] a week.

I shall be pleased to have your recommendations. Since I plan to be in Boston on April 12,[8] I shall be glad to talk with any of your students who are interested. Sincerely yours, (177)

26▶ Dear Mr. Gold: I have selected five undergraduate students who are worthy of your consideration[1] for the jobs connected with your marketing study. These students will be available to talk with you when you[2] come to Boston on April 12.

Please let me know what time you plan to arrive on the campus and how much time you[3] expect to spend with each student. Just as soon as I have this information, I shall prepare a schedule of[4] interviews. Three of these young people have jobs, and it is important for them to know when they are to see you.

I[5] believe you will find these five people willing workers. All are students in our Business Department and therefore have[6] had courses in typewriting and business machines. Very truly yours, (133)

* * *

▶ Always fill in the subject line on an interoffice memorandum. This will make the memorandum easier to read and to file.

part

2

UNITS 2-12▶ Lessons 6-60

Secretarial Assignment

1 A study of all phases of the association's work would be beneficial.

2 During the probationary period no appraisal of your office procedures is scheduled.

3 If a member of the Personnel Department helped you in handling employee interviews, you would undoubtedly reciprocate.

4 A number of inquiries are similar in scope and should be discounted.

5 To avoid obsolescence, don't buy large quantities of materials.

6 As an accommodation, we are sending the recommendation to your representative.

7 We are inaugurating schedule innovations and should appreciate your cooperation.

8 Is it appropriate to ask why you are disappointed in our plan for a home-conveniences display?

LESSON 6

1 His decision to reject the report was clear cut.

2 He adopted an out-of-reach objective to motivate his staff.

3 An early morning conference was scheduled for Tuesday.

4 The proposal would have far-reaching effects on the plan.

5 This is a fairly clear explanation of a difficult problem.

6 The 14-page report was presented to the rules committee.

7 The competition conducted a campaign by direct mail.

8 He is a self-made man, and he has solved many problems.

9 His position during the meeting is hard to understand.

10 His preparation for the class made him self-reliant.

27▶ Mr. William R. Browne, American Management Association, 135 West 50 Street, New York, New York 10019.

Dear Bill: Thank you for inviting me to participate in the workshop on automation to be held on June[1] 13 and 14. I shall be happy to accept the invitation.

From previous experiences with[2] AMA workshops, I know that you prefer unstructured programs; therefore, I will follow your usual pattern. In[3] the course of the two days, though, I hope to describe the experiences of our own company during the[4] transition to computers, including the retraining of workers whose skills became obsolescent, the early[5] retirement of workers who did not wish to learn new techniques, and the changes in our requirements for personnel.

Since[6] we have been disappointed in the reaction of some of our most loyal employees to early retirement,[7] I hope to make inquiries about how other companies have handled this difficult problem.

I note from[8] your letter that you plan to hold a meeting of program participants before the workshop gets under way. Please[9] let me know the time and place of that meeting immediately so that I will know how long I shall have to be[10] away from my job here.

I am looking forward to working with you on this program. Sincerely yours, (218)

28▶ Mr. Harold P. Myers, Management Consultant, Hayes, Myers, and Wilson Company, New Rochelle, New York 10802.

Dear Harold: Your paper at the annual convention of the Systems and Procedures Association on[1] developing standards for choosing your duplicating equipment as well as methods of training your office[2] personnel to select the appropriate process was most beneficial to me.

I wonder whether you have[3] additional reprints of the paper. Although you provided a large supply of copies of the talk for[4] distribution to the audience at last week's meeting, the supply was not large enough to accommodate all who[5] wanted them. If you do not have copies of the entire speech, perhaps you can send me the portion of the talk that[6] was taken from your training manual for supervisors.

If you will make this material available[7] to me, may I have permission to include it in our own training manual? It would improve our handling of[8] materials requiring wide distribution and would prevent the supervisors from making unwise choices[9] of duplicating equipment for various kinds of jobs. Equally important, it would require them to rely[10] on facts

rather than on generalities.

Enclosed is a copy of the Guide to Reproduction Processes[11] that I drafted for our supervisors. It helps them to select the duplicating process that will give them[12] the right balance of cost, appearance, and durability. Your reactions, please! Sincerely, (257)

29▶ To: Edward R. Harmon, Director, Personnel Department, Subject: Employee Appraisal.

I should like to make the following recommendations:

1. That we inaugurate long-range plans for developing[1] an employee-appraisal system.

2. That we utilize the findings of the Systems and Procedures Unit[2] regarding quality and quantity of work produced in the various clerical, typist, and stenographic[3] classifications when they become available.

3. That we solicit recommendations for such a[4] system from personnel officers belonging to the national organizations.

4. That your unit make[5] a library study of research in this field.

5. That, after we have gone as far with the plan as we can go,[6] we can consider employing a management consultant to help develop an effective system. I shall[7] be glad to discuss these proposals with you at your convenience. (152)

LESSON 7

30▶ The Acme Letter Service, 117 East Madison Street, Boston, Massachusetts 02178.

Gentlemen: We should like to explore the possibility of using a letter service for the production[1] and distribution of our direct-mail sales letters.

At the present time we use automatic typewriters[2] capable of producing letters that cannot be distinguished from original ones. We believe, however, that[3] letter costs might be reduced if we used an outside agency, such as yours, for handling our direct mail. Another[4] reason for our interest is the strong feeling that you may be able to provide better prospect lists than[5] those developed by our salesmen. We need lists that would contain more recent addresses than ours, lists that would contain[6] more active prospects than we seem to reach. Our salesmen simply do not have the facilities for updating mailing[7] lists outside their immediate territory. As a result, we are undoubtedly sending direct mail[8] to wrong addresses and to many people who are no longer potential customers.

Before we can complete[9] a preliminary analysis of our present direct-mail costs, we need answers to four questions.

1. What[10] is the cost per thousand of a 150-word sales message addressed by you from our lists?

2. What is the[11] cost if addressed by you from your lists?

3. What is your source of a national prospect list for our product?

4. How[12] often is such a list updated?

We need to study your an-swers to these questions before we invite you to[13] meet with us to explore further the possibility of your handling our direct-mail advertising. Sincerely[14] yours, (281)

31▶ Mr. Harold K. Putnam, Office Manager, Springer Manufacturing Corporation, Wilmington, Delaware 19804.

Dear Mr. Putnam: Our lively discussion of office problems during the recent American Management[1] Association's national convention was the highlight of my Chicago sojourn. I enjoyed it immensely[2] and profited greatly from talking over employee-rating problems with somebody from a company[3] similar to NATIONAL PRODUCTS in organization.

You mentioned that you appraise employee performance[4] on a quarterly basis. Will you please send me a sample of the appraisal form that you use. It would be[5] beneficial to me if you would explain which employees are rated and whether they are rated by more than one[6] person.

Enclosed is a self-appraisal form I developed for our middle-management people. They are asked to[7] rate themselves prior to the scheduled interview with the person they report to, who has just completed their[8] annual appraisal. Sincerely yours, (167)

32▶ To: Director of Systems and Procedures, Subject: Work-Measurement Study.

The time has come to inaugurate a plan for measuring both the quality and the quantity of work[1] produced by clerks, typists, and stenographers employed by Administrative Services. There is too wide a[2] variation in both the amount and the kind of clerical and stenographic work turned out. Frankly, we need[3] reliable time standards.

Will you please take the necessary steps to schedule a work-measurement study that[4] would help me to distribute the existing work load fairly, identify reasonable job standards, and pinpoint[5] critical areas where additional help is justified. (113)

33▸ To: Mary Williamson, Supervisor, Women's Personnel Services, Subject: Voluntary Separations.

We have had a disturbing number of voluntary separations among our stenographers and secretaries[1] during the last six months. Inasmuch as you conduct exit interviews with all stenographic and[2] secretarial personnel leaving National Products, you can help me to pinpoint areas of dissatisfaction.[3]

Of course, it is not likely that the real reasons for separation are always given when inquiries[4] are made. It would be beneficial to me, however, if I could have a photocopy of your exit[5] interview with the following secretaries:

1. Helen Ann Bruce
2. Natalie R. Martinson
3. Barbara[6] Ellen Knox

If I read these reports, perhaps I can identify the features of work in Administrative[7] Services that stenographers and secretaries dislike. Then I will try to inaugurate appropriate[8] changes that will improve conditions and thus decrease this costly turnover. (174)

LESSON 8

34▸ To: Employees in Administrative Services, Subject: Coffee Breaks.

You will be glad to know that we have contracted with Essential Restaurant Services to supply coffee, tea,[1] milk, and pastries each day between 10 and 11 a.m. and between 3 and 4 p.m. Their facilities[2] include portable wagons that will stop at designated stations near your desks, where you can enjoy a 15-[3]minute break.

The reasons we think you will be pleased are these: (1) the coffee break will be free to all employees, and[4] (2) you will not waste your coffee-break time waiting for elevators to take you to the cafeteria.

We[5] hope you will be pleased with this new system, which is being adopted for your convenience. (116)

35▸ To: Mildred Emmons, Supervisor, Stenographic Pool, Subject: Revision of Office Manual.

This is an invitation to become a member of a committee to revise the company's office[1] manual. As you have often expressed the need to standardize the style for correspondence throughout National Products,[2] you will undoubtedly approve of the project and want to participate in it.

As supervisor of[3] the stenographic pool, you have a real contribution to make. I shall rely on you to identify[4] office practices that represent modern usage. At the same time, we must try to reduce office costs to a[5] greater extent than is possible with the current office manual.

I shall serve as chairman of the committee.[6] Just as soon as I hear from all prospective members, I shall convene the group so that we can plan a revision[7] schedule. In the meantime, Mildred, would you write to a number of other companies and ask them for copies[8] of their office manuals. They may be a valuable source for new ideas. (176)

36▶ Mr. William Workman, Sales Manager, Consolidated Files, 220 State Street, Duluth, Minnesota 55803.

Dear Mr. Workman: We have been experiencing difficulty in filing our edge-punched computer cards. They[1] seem to buckle while they are stored, even though we keep them in the special file you sold us for protecting computer[2] cards. They will not feed into the computer in this condition.

We have had so much trouble that we wonder[3] whether you should send someone to look into the situation. On the other hand, perhaps you can make a[4]

recommendation by mail.

The difficulty may be caused by our placing the files in the wrong location. As you[5] remember, they are not in the air-conditioned area. Do you think that their efficiency is being[6] affected by humidity? If you recommend that we move the files to a more appropriate spot in the[7] air-conditioned computer room, we shall do so immediately. If you feel that the location of the files is[8] not the reason for the difficulty and are undecided about a solution to the problem, then we[9] shall expect a representative to visit us to make an appropriate recommendation. Yours very[10] truly, (201)

37▶ The Progressive Office Supply Company, 214 State Street, Chicago, Illinois 60610.

Gentlemen: This morning we received the 50,000 envelopes that we ordered on July 19. We are,[1] however, disappointed with the quality. Our supervisor tells me that the envelopes do not match the[2] letterheads you supplied last month. This inferior quality is useless to us, and we wonder what you plan[3] to do about the order.

We have not had a similar experience during all the years you have been handling[4] our orders, and we feel sure that you will want to make an adjustment. I suggest that your salesman come in soon[5] to work out a satisfactory settlement. Yours very truly, (112)

38▶ Reliable Typewriter Com-

pany, 4320 Madison Road, Hartford, Connecticut 06101, Attention of Mr. Edgar Walters.

Gentlemen: Our typewriter service contract will expire on November 8. At that time we shall be able to[1] order 25 new electric typewriters to replace obsolescent manual machines. Before we place[2] the order, however, we should like to make inquiries of all typewriter sales representatives about their[3] quotations on the yearly service contracts.

We feel that we are now paying too high a rate for keeping our machines[4] in first-class condition. Since we shall be adding 25 new machines, your service engineers will undoubtedly[5] spend much less time maintaining each machine than is now the case.

Your quotation on a new service contract[6] will influence our choice of new electric machines. Cordially yours, (132)

LESSON 9

43▶ Professor Helen Norton, Chairman, Department of Business Education, Eastern University, Worcester, Massachusetts 01601.

Dear Professor Norton: Thank you for inviting me to speak to your students about the opportunities in the[1] field of business. I can arrange to visit your campus on February 7. If I come directly to your[2] office from the train station, I should be able to make my presentation at ten o'clock. Thank you also for[3] your thoughtful invitation to lunch with the faculty members who are free at twelve o'clock.

The title of my[4] talk will be "Competing with a Computer in the World of Work." The relationship between employability[5] and education will be stressed.

You may be sure that the value of secretarial training will be emphasized,[6] for it is one field of endeavor that does not face serious obsolescence. This job classification[7] will probably be upgraded while machines are displacing clerks at lower levels.

I shall describe some of[8] the new job categories that are developing. Some job categories that will be attractive to your college[9] students are as follows: Programmer, systems analyst, management consultant, transcription supervisor,[10] correspondent, and office manager.

If you have additional suggestions for my talk, please feel free to extend[11] them. Sincerely yours, (224)

44▶ Mr. John Cramer, Manager, Progressive Office Employment Services, 3479 State Street, Chicago, Illinois 60626.

Dear John: Our Personnel Department has not been able to employ a satisfactory trainee for an unfilled[1] systems-analysis position.

Perhaps you know of a young college graduate with a background in business[2] administration who would have the abilities we want. A person who

16

meets the job specifications set[3] up by the Administrative Management Association would probably satisfy our needs.

If you have[4] a recommendation, please send it to Edward R. Harmon, director of our Personnel Department. I have[5] told him to expect a suggestion from your agency by the end of this week. Cordially yours, (118)

45▶ To: Edward R. Harmon, Director, Personnel Section, Subject: Systems-Analyst Trainee.

I am disappointed, Ed, that you have not been able to locate a suitable trainee in systems analysis.[1]

As you suggested, I have just sent a request to John Cramer, at Progressive Office Employment Services,[2] for a young college graduate to fill this vacancy. We shall probably have to be satisfied with[3] an inexperienced man.

As you know, I have been associated with John for a long time in the Administrative[4] Management Association; I think that he can help us. I asked him to send anyone he recommends[5] directly to you. (103)

46▶ Mr. Bernard Lange, World-Wide Office Equipment Company, 332 Randolph Street, Chicago, Illinois 60610.

Dear Mr. Lange: We are interested in purchasing several photocopy machines. In my opinion,[1] we should have at least two machines on each floor in Administrative Services so that no secretary will[2] spend time in copying letters that can better be photographed. These machines will undoubtedly increase the production[3] of all employees in the unit, for they will speed material on its way that would otherwise be delayed[4] until the secretary found time to copy it.

We have studied the circulars and newspaper advertisements[5] of several manufacturers and have asked them to let us see their demonstration machines in our office.[6] We should like to extend an invitation to you to show your photocopy machine so that we can try[7] it for a short period. Yours very truly, (148)

LESSON 10

48▶ Mr. William C. Howard, Office Manager, Bedford Manufacturing Corporation, 4352 Washington Avenue, Bedford, Massachusetts 01730.

Dear Mr. Howard: Thank you for your comments about my article in the December issue of Administrative[1] Management on problems of developing the employee during his probationary period[2] of employment. Your approval means a great deal to me because of your own beneficial contributions to[3] the field of personnel and office management. I have received numerous inquiries similar to yours since[4] the article was published.

Here at NATIONAL PRODUCTS every new employee assigned to Administrative[5] Services understands that he is on probation for six months and that he may be discharged if we are[6] disappointed in his work or in his job attitude. On the other hand, we feel responsibility for the[7] successful induction of the new employee into all phases of his work. He receives a briefing on standard[8] office practices in Administrative Services by his supervisor who goes through the office[9] manual with him before presenting it to him as a desk reference.

Although the employee's supervisor[10] is primarily responsible for his successful induction, a weekly class session lasting two hours is[11] conducted by our Training Department for all workers employed within a six-week period. At these sessions[12] the history of the company, its organization, and its products are explained. The workers are encouraged[13] at these sessions to ask any questions they may have. In addition, the supervisor reports to the Training[14] Department any phases of work done by the probationary worker that do not measure up to company[15] standards. The new worker may be assigned to classes for as many as two hours a day during the[16] probationary period. In this way we overcome any loss of skills experienced by the worker since his last[17] employment. We also make him aware of any variations in standard office procedures from those of[18] previous employers.

At the end of six months the work of the probationary employee is reviewed by his[19] supervisor and by me. We consider the quality and quantity of work produced and the compatibility[20] of the employee with his fellow workers. The supervisor and I discuss the appraisal and[21] decide whether the worker is to be put on the permanent payroll or whether he will be a liability[22] to the company.

We have found that we have reduced the number of job terminations by 30 percent[23] since we inaugurated this plan two years ago. We believe in it. If you decide to make innovations[24] in your handling of probationary workers, Mr. Howard, I should appreciate your telling me about[25] them. Sincerely yours, (503)

* * *

▶ A tip to left-handed writers: You may find it more convenient to write your notes first in the second column of your notebook and then in the first column. The "upside-down" left-handed writer should turn the book upside down, with the spiral at the bottom, so that it does not get in his way.

Unit 3————————

Secretarial Assignment

1 We appreciate your conscientious efforts to reimburse us.
2 The bookkeeper accidentally forgot to send an acknowledgment.
3 Incidentally, your sizable check enabled us to meet our financial obligations.

4 It is a joy to work with attorneys who are both courteous and efficient.

5 Failure to meet your financial obligations will jeopardize your credit privilege.

6 The exorbitant fees of some attorneys may have a disastrous effect on their professional image.

7 We occasionally allow an extension of the discount period for conscientious customers when they give a plausible explanation for their delinquency.

8 Maintenance of a good credit standing is indispensable to efficient operation.

9 The financial welfare of the customer is always a conscientious consideration in every credit transaction.

10 Credit is a privilege rather than a right, and it should be used discreetly.

LESSON 11

1 Definite, clear-cut information is the basis for extending credit.

2 You improve your credit standing when you pay bills promptly.

3 Because punctuation is basic, you should master it now.

4 We bought a new key-driven calculator yesterday.

5 When it becomes necessary, attorneys are asked to collect overdue bills.

6 Marvin Green is a young business executive.

7 A secretary should master punctuation because it is a vital tool.

8 If a customer is a poor risk, he receives frequent collection letters.

9 Miss Carter is an efficient, dependable employee.

10 We have developed a simplified, faster system of billing.

49▶ Mr. Harry Morris, President, The Morris Company, 144 Grand Avenue, Kansas City, Missouri 64100.

Dear Mr. Morris: When you made application for credit a few months ago, we made the usual investigation[1] among your creditors and examined carefully your most recent financial statements. All reports[2] were consistently favorable, and credit was extended to you. The limit of $5,000 was[3] unusually high for a new customer.

We are beginning to wonder, however, what has occurred[4] since credit privileges were established for you. You have owed us $3,248 for[5] four months, and you have repeatedly ignored our statements and reminders. Incidentally, if you had paid your[6] account according to the accepted terms, 2/10, n/30, you would have earned a discount of $64.96.[7]

As manufacturers of nationally advertised products, we are interested in the[8] welfare of our distributors and in their credit reputation with the entire business community.[9] Actually, they represent us. As you know, the national agencies regularly ask us to supply credit[10] information about our customers. I am afraid that at this moment our report on you would not be[11] a favorable one.

With this thought in mind, we urge you to mail your check today — before you jeopardize your credit[12] standing further. Sincerely yours, (247)

50▶ The Brownlee Company, Box 614, Tulsa, Oklahoma 74122.

Gentlemen: When you did not pay the $3,175 outstanding on our Invoice[1] TY7302 by January 15, you lost the 5 percent trade discount that would have saved you[2] $158.75. At the time, we were surprised; but we assumed it was a bookkeeper's[3] oversight, for you have seldom missed the opportunity to earn your discounts.

When you did not pay this[4] sizable account at the end of January, we were again surprised, for we know that you wouldn't willingly[5] jeopardize your excellent credit reputation.

When you did not respond to two reminders that your account[6] is overdue, we were surprised for the third time.

Perhaps your delay in paying this bill is due to the mild, disconcerting[7] recession the business community is experiencing. If this is the case, we should like to[8] talk over your financial situation with you. If you prefer, we can accommodate you by giving you[9] an extension of time or by arranging a sequence of regular payments that will permit you to reduce[10] this outstanding account.

We hope you will interpret this courteous request as a sincere effort to help you[11] to meet your financial obligations.

Yours very truly, (231)

51▶ Mr. Edward Milbank, Milbank Mercantile Company, Bound Brook, New Jersey 08805.

Dear Mr. Milbank: Although we may seem persistent, we do want the $348.19[1] you have owed us since April 5. We also want to continue being friends with you, Mr. Milbank. Our business[2] relationship during the past two years has been mutually beneficial. Certainly we have appreciated[3] the opportunity to satisfy your needs. You have benefited, we trust, by the quality of our[4] products, our favorable prices, and our dependable delivery schedules.

Until recently your record[5] for prompt payment had been unblemished. For this reason we suspect that there must be some good reason for the nonpayment[6] of your account. If we have billed you incorrectly, we want to know about it so that we can make the[7] necessary adjustments.

On the other hand, if your inability to pay this account is caused by a[8] financial problem, perhaps we can help you work out a satisfactory solution that will enable you[9] to reduce your present indebtedness. We want to continue to ship merchandise to you and help you maintain[10] your necessary inventory levels. We must, however, have your immediate cooperation if[11] we are to work together effectively. May we hear from you within five days? Sincerely yours, (237)

LESSON 12

52▶ Ace Stop and Save, 161 Locust Street, Bowling Green, Ohio 43401.

Gentlemen: As we have not received a reply to any of our four letters requesting payment of your overdue[1] account, we must assume that you do not intend to take any action. We are therefore instructing our attorneys[2] to proceed with collection of the bill.

Naturally, we are disturbed that you have chosen to disregard[3] our courteous requests for settlement and thereby jeopardize your credit standing. Some explanation from[4] you would have made this drastic step unnecessary. Your complete silence, however, has left us no other course[5] of action. Yours very truly, (105)

53▶ The Goodman Manufacturing Company, 1411 Tenth Avenue, Amarillo, Texas 79104.

Gentlemen: Will you please tell us your experience in selling on credit to the firm whose name appears on the[1] attached form. In asking for credit, the applicant used your company as a reference.

It would be extremely[2] helpful if you would indicate whether you consider this company to be enterprising, whether you[3] have ever been dissatisfied in your dealings with it, and whether you have had an uninterrupted relationship[4] with it. We have found that such general information about a customer is frequently worth more[5]

than a technical analysis of his financial condition.

All disclosures you make, of course, will be kept[6] confidential. Please use the convenient form at the bottom of this letter to transmit the information we[7] need. Yours very truly, (144)

54▶ Mr. Todd F. Bradford, Bradford-Heaton, Inc., 3 East Willow Street, Bowling Green, Ohio 43402.

Dear Mr. Bradford: I hope that the products you ordered from us for sale during the spring season moved well and that[1] you profited from having them shipped early on open account for this special event. We were glad to accommodate[2] you, for we understand the importance of timing.

Timing is important to us, too, in terms of our[3] own obligations. As you know, we have not received payment of your invoice; and this payment was expected over[4] a month ago. Apparently, our two previous reminders went astray.

You know that you can depend on[5] us to supply you with quality products promptly. We believe we have a right to expect that you will carry[6] out your part of the bargain by making payment promptly. Your overdue invoice amounts to $791.23.[7] Won't you send us your check immediately? We shall appreciate it. Sincerely[8] yours, (161)

55▶ Mr. George H. Martin, Executive Vice-President, Martin-Simpson Company, Box 404,

Trenton, New Jersey 08605.

Dear Mr. Martin: You earn credit in much the same way that you earn the respect of your neighbors or the admiration[1] of your family.

Six months ago you were granted the privilege of buying merchandise for your store[2] on a credit basis. A routine check of your financial ability and consistency in paying your[3] bills prompted us to include you among our credit customers.

Now you are jeopardizing your credit privilege[4] by not paying a balance of $1,773.12, the total of[5] Invoices 83J, 174E, and 361Y. The first of these invoices is more than 60[6] days past due, and the other two are over 30 days past due.

Furthermore, you have not responded to three reminder[7] letters. Unless you honor this obligation in full or arrange for a systematic reduction[8] of this debt, you may find it extremely difficult to retain a favorable credit position. Unpaid[9] accounts such as yours are referred to me before being turned over to our attorneys for collection. Although[10] legal fees are expensive, the disastrous effect such action would have on your credit standing is even more[11] expensive.

If you choose not to make satisfactory arrangements to settle this account within five days, Mr.[12] Martin, we shall have to take legal steps to obtain a settlement. Yours very truly, (257)

56▶ Mr. James C. Perry, Manager, The Associated Shops,

1411 Jefferson Street, Elgin, Illinois 60122.

Dear Mr. Perry: Much as we should like to ship your order of February 18 on open account, Mr.[1] Perry, we are not in a position to do so. Our routine credit investigation reveals insufficient[2] favorable information about your financial condition; therefore, we must obtain more data.[3]

While we are obtaining this credit information, may we ship your order on a C.O.D. basis? I know[4] you need the furnishings immediately to take care of your customer demands, and we can make shipment just[5] as soon as we receive your assurance that you will accept it on C.O.D. terms. Incidentally, you[6] automatically earn a 3 percent discount under this arrangement.

We shall look forward to hearing from you.[7] Yours very truly, (143)

* * *

▶ When your shorthand notebook is filled, indicate on the cover the ending date of the material contained. Of course, you entered the beginning date when you started the notebook.

LESSON 13

57▶ Memo to: Henry D. Walters, Vice-President — Finance, Subject: Report on Collections.

On Monday of this week you asked me for information about the status of our collections of money due[1] so that you can predict the cash needs of National Products for the next three months. The following information[2] is based on an analysis that has just been completed of all current accounts now stored on magnetic[3] tape. It covers all transactions during the interval from January 1 through May 31 .

Bills turned over[4] to attorneys 2%.

Bills uncollected by attorneys 1%.

Bills outstanding 31 to 60[5] days 15%.

Bills outstanding 11 to 30 days 17%.

Bills collected within[6] 10-day discount period 37%.

Goods sold for cash 28%.

It is worth noting that[7] our percentage of uncollected bills is at an all-time low. We have, however, slipped from 47 percent[8] to 37 percent in the bills paid during the 2/10, n/30 discount period. This figure[9] means that our cash on hand will have to be increased 10 percent if we are going to be able to take our own[10] cash discounts.

I have tried to interest our most active accounts in taking their discounts automatically,[11] but my efforts have been hampered by the international political situation and the general[12] sluggish condition of business.

I shall welcome any suggestions you may have, Mr. Walters, for raising the[13] percentage of customers taking their discounts within the 10-day period. (274)

58▸ Memo to: John Parker, Director of Administrative Services, Subject: Form Letters for Credit Correspondence.

I believe, John, that too much time is spent by credit correspondents in dictating credit and collection letters.[1] Many of these letters, especially collection letters, cover the same or almost identical[2] situations; yet each is now being dictated individually. It seems to me that we could save much time,[3] money, and effort if we developed form letters for routine collection situations. These form letters would[4] provide blank spaces for individual fill-ins of date, name, amount, and invoice number.

Could your department[5] duplicate these letters for us? All the credit correspondent would have to do, in many situations, is[6] tell the clerk-typist the number of the letter he wishes used and give her the fill-in information. Probably[7] one clerk-typist, working at an automatic typewriter, could take care of the needs of two or three correspondents.[8] We would probably call on your department to supply the clerk-typist, and her salary would be paid[9] by the Credit Department.

I am also thinking of writing special paragraphs that could be substituted[10] in letters where a fill-in would not serve the purpose. In this case, we would tell the clerk-typist to use, for example,[11] Paragraph 1 from Code A, Paragraph 2 from Code C, and so on. This would greatly simplify our correspondence[12] problems.

Perhaps we ought to discuss this suggestion and how it might be worked out between us. A meeting[13] of the key people in our departments might be very profitable. How about next Wednesday at 10 a.m. in[14] the Conference Room? (283)

59▶ Mr. Willard M. Ewing, Credit Manager, The Standard Chemical Company, 704 West Avenue, Milwaukee, Wisconsin 53289.

Dear Willard: You asked about the time schedule we use for letters in our collection series. I am glad to give[1] you our plan, although I know you realize that it might not work for you. I have found that no company's collection[2] policy can be modeled completely on that of another organization.

As you know, all accounts[3] do not carry the same risk and should not be handled alike. For practical purposes, we classify our accounts[4] into three categories: poor risks, fair risks, and good risks.

Poor risks receive fewer communications than others[5] because we have found that they must be dealt with quickly and decisively. No more than five reminders are sent.[6] A statement is sent at the beginning of the month following purchase. If no response is received by the 15th,[7] a letter is sent asking whether the customer was displeased with the goods. At the end of another fifteen[8] days a

letter is written stressing the fairness of the request for payment. After the next fifteen days[9] another letter goes out emphasizing the importance of a good credit rating. The final appeal, along[10] with the statement that the bill will be turned over to a collection agency, is sent after the final fifteen[11] days — three months after the debt was incurred.

Fair risks receive more communications. Usually two statements[12] are sent before a letter is written. A third statement is then mailed with a note attached that says the bill has[13] presumably been overlooked. After these reminders, the cycle described above is followed. Communications[14] are sent every fifteen days, and the collection procedure may take up to four months.

Good risks receive up to[15] nine communications. There may be as many as four statements, the last one accompanied by a note. The letters[16] increasingly emphasize the serious consequences of jeopardizing a good credit rating. Eventually[17] a deadline is specified, when the attorneys or collection agency will take over; but this[18] deadline may be delayed up to five months, with some type of communication reaching the customer every[19] fifteen days.

I must emphasize that a credit man should avoid using a stereotyped set of letters. He[20] must always consider his job a challenging one and must introduce creativity into his letters[21] at

24

every opportunity. Cordially yours, (430)

64▶ Memo to: Mr. Philip Irwin, Manager, Subject: Computer Billing.

Our system of computerized accounting for sales seems to be working out well so far as the Collection[1] Department is concerned. We get our lists of delinquent accounts more quickly than ever before; this permits us to[2] summarize our collection data within an hour or two after receiving a request for information.[3] We get a print-out of overdue accounts every Monday, grouped into three categories: bills overdue[4] more than 60 days, bills overdue 31 to 60 days, and bills overdue 11 to 30 days.[5] A separate list of customers who took advantage of 10-day discounts is also enclosed.

We are, however,[6] experiencing considerable difficulty by not having accounts updated immediately[7] after payments have been received. Several customers have been displeased because they received a statement for a[8] bill already paid.

I believe that changes in programming should be introduced that will update more quickly the[9] information already stored on the magnetic tape. (190)

65▶ Mr. Donald Adams, The Adams Shoppe, Winchester Road, Mount Vernon, New York 10551.

Dear Mr. Adams: I have just circled September 15 on my desk calendar. I suggest that you circle[1] the 14th, for that's the day your check for $217.11 must be mailed to reach us[2] on the 15th. Unless your check is received on that circled date, I shall be forced to turn your account over to[3] our attorneys for collection.

We realize, as no doubt you do, Mr. Adams, the serious effect this[4] step will have on your credit standing. There is a way that you can prevent this action. Either mail your check so that[5] we shall receive it by September 15, or send us a letter or telegram telling us your plans for payment.[6] Yours very truly, (123)

66▶ Mr. Harry R. Mason, Mason & Brown, 145 Shelton Drive, Wilmington, Delaware 19814.

Dear Mr. Mason: Thank you, Mr. Mason, for your response to our request for payment.

Your check for the entire[1] amount due and your courteous explanation of the delay are appreciated. We welcome future[2] opportunities to be of service. Sincerely yours, (50)

67▶ Mr. Walter C. Edgar, Edgar Retail Shop, Bowden Square, Portland, Maine 04110.

Dear Mr. Edgar: We are wondering why we have not received your check for $423.45[1] in payment of our Invoice No. 43332.

Let's review the situation: The bill was due[2] on February 17. You did not pay it or tell us why. We sent you another statement on March[3] 1. Again we did not receive your check. We wrote you on March 15 and asked whether something was wrong with the way[4] we handled the shipment or the billing. As of today, March 31, we have had no reply to that letter[5] either.

In fairness to us and to yourself, Mr. Edgar, won't you get in touch with us immediately. Either[6] send us the check or tell us your plans for payment. Yours very truly, (133)

68▶ Alfred Williams, Inc., Fairfield Shopping Center, Phoenix, Arizona 85013.

Gentlemen: Your check for $375 in payment of our Invoice No. 1113[1] should have reached us on March 16. It is now May 1, and we still have not received it nor have we had an explanation[2] from you as to why it was not sent.

Because our business dealings over the years have been so pleasant and[3] mutually profitable, I feel certain that something has happened in your business that accounts for your delay[4] in meeting your obligations. Won't you tell us what it is? No doubt we can work out something satisfactory[5] to both of us.

Please let me hear from you immediately. The fact that our three previous reminders have[6] been ignored disturbs me greatly. Is it possible that you did not receive them? Cordially yours, (137)

70▶ Mr. William Metzler, Metzler Variety Store, Meadowlark Shopping Center, Greeley, Colorado 80630.

Dear Mr. Metzler: Our accountant has just credited your payment of August 8 to your account. In doing[1] so, he called my attention to the conscientious way in which you have always met your financial obligations.[2]

Thank you, Mr. Metzler, for your patronage and for your splendid way of doing business. NATIONAL PRODUCTS[3] considers it a privilege to have you as a customer. We look forward to many opportunities[4] of serving you, Cordially yours, (86)

71▶ Mr. Elmer L. Dewitt, Dewitt Manufacturing Company, 141 East Chapel Street, Harrison, New Jersey 07029.

Dear Mr. Dewitt: We are happy to tell you our experience in selling on credit to the Square D[1] Company of Piping Rock, Arkansas.

We have had continuous dealings with this company for the past eleven[2] years. In fact, we extended credit to Mr. Hastings, the founder, when he first entered business. We have watched[3] the company grow from a small country store into a sizable department store with annual sales totaling[4] $200,000. Recently it has added lines from tropical fish to mechanical toys, from[5] musical instruments to men's furnishings.

We have always had a high regard for Mr. Hastings and his[6] conscientious handling of the financial affairs of his company. During the eight years that he headed the company,[7] he usually took his discounts; and we received most of our payments on time. When he was occasionally[8] a little slow, he would explain the delay and ask for an extension. He always deserved an A-plus[9] credit rating.

During the past three years, though, a change has occurred. This is a family-owned business, and the two[10] Hastings sons have now entered the management. Perhaps they have become too diversified or have introduced too[11] many innovations. In any event, we have not been as pleased with our relations with the Square D Company[12] as we were in previous years. The sons have not been as conscientious as their father in paying their bills and[13] in earning discounts. Occasionally they attempt to take unearned discounts. Too frequently they defer payments[14] until we exert considerable pressure to collect. We have heard rumors of some disagreement between[15] the brothers.

In all fairness, though, we must tell you that the uncertainties seem to be decreasing. Payments have become[16] more regular in the last two months, and our attitude is correspondingly less critical. None of the[17] unpaid balance today is overdue. We have heard that the older brother has assumed control.

This detailed,[18] confidential interpretation of the situation at the Square D Company is given because we feel[19] that the conditions are rather unusual. We are confident that the brothers have resolved their problems, and[20] we intend to continue granting credit up to $2,000. As a precaution, however, we shall[21] run a systematic check on their pattern of payments.

We hope that this information is beneficial. Cordially[22] yours, (441)

*   *   *

▶ Be sure to leave a few blank lines between each letter in your shorthand notebook. This will not only help you to judge the length of each letter for transcription purposes, but it will allow room for any special instructions regarding the correspondence (number of carbon copies, special mailing or handling procedures, etc).

Unit 4

Secretarial Assignment

1 Are you familiar with the pamphlet describing careers in business?
2 I am optimistic about not misspelling this list of miscellaneous words.
3 How do you gauge your chances of locating a plant in this vicinity?
4 He separated the mediocre workers from those showing initiative.
5 By unanimous vote the group chose new rules to supersede the old ones.

6 We are vying with other manufacturers in a highly competitive market.
7 We are wholly in agreement with the consensus of the managers.
8 Attendance at the meeting was high, with few absences.
9 His abilities are so versatile that he is eligible for promotion.
10 We maintain liaison with several agencies that produce acceptable advertisements.

LESSON 16

1 Employee benefits include stock-purchase plans, insurance, and bonuses.
2 They discussed the plan but did not adopt it.
3 We provide training inside the company and with outside colleges.
4 He prepared the manual, but he was not satisfied with it.
5 A few employees read the manual, put it in their desks, and never refer to it again.
6 The manager's secretary types, files, and checks figures but seldom operates the photocopier.
7 Our supply of erasers, pencils, and notebooks is low.
8 Employee motivation is a problem both in the plant and in the office.
9 He interviewed, tested, and hired an office force in one week.
10 The inexperience of the employee and the lack of proper supervision were given as reasons for the mistake.

72▶ **Mr. Richard D. Beatty, 1401 Sheridan Road, Wilmette, Illinois 60091.**

Dear Mr. Beatty: I am happy to tell you that you have been chosen for the position of administrative[1] assistant to Mr. Charles C. Haynes, director of Research and Development, at a salary of[2] $8,500. I realize that this is less than you had hoped to receive, but it is in line with[3] salaries paid in comparable positions here. You know, of course, that our median salary for middle[4] management personnel is one of the highest in the area. In addition, salaries are reviewed[5] every six months; so you may feel optimistic about opportunities for advancement.

Your reporting[6] date will be September 1. This will permit you to give two weeks' notice to your present employer, and it will[7] also give you a week's vacation before taking on your new responsibilities.

Mr. Haynes and his staff[8] are looking forward to your arrival. Please send your written acceptance at once. We wish to make a number of[9] preliminary arrangements that will expedite your induction. Sincerely yours, (195)

73▶ **Miss Elizabeth Drew, 1411 Wacker Drive, Chicago, Illinois 60613.**

Dear Miss Drew: We have reviewed your performance ratings, your attendance record, and your test scores covering your[1] probationary period of six months; and we are happy to tell you that you will become a permanent[2] employee as of July 18.

You are now eligible for acceptance into our pension system. If you[3] wish to discuss your rate of contribution, please see William Rifkin in the Payroll Department.

Another employee[4] benefit for which you are now eligible is our stock-purchase plan. You may buy shares in your company[5] at reduced rates on a salary-withholding schedule.

We are optimistic, Miss Drew, about your future[6] with NATIONAL PRODUCTS. If at any time you wish to discuss your career plans, please feel free to see me or a[7] member of my staff. Yours cordially, (147)

74▶ Mr. Robert E. Robinson, Howard Dormitory, University of Arizona, Tucson, Arizona 85721.

Dear Mr. Robinson: Thank you for the interest you have shown in obtaining a position in the international[1] sales division of NATIONAL PRODUCTS. Mr. Arthur Johnson has forwarded your application[2] and a report of his interview with you on the campus of the University of Arizona. He[3] feels that your qualifications come close to meeting the requirements of our international sales division.[4]

Therefore, Mr. Robinson, we should like to have you visit us here in St. Louis for further interviews. We[5] also want you to take a special battery of tests that we routinely administer to all candidates[6] for positions in sales. This procedure would require two days and would be at our expense. If convenient to you,[7] we suggest the dates of June 2 and 3.

Actually, Mr. Robinson, we are considering several[8] candidates for this position. Because we must make a considerable investment in each new sales employee,[9] we shall consider each person very carefully before making a choice. However, your academic[10] standing, your facility in speaking Spanish, and your versatile sales experience in your father's sporting[11] supply store have led us to believe you are a young man with great promise.

Please let me know immediately whether[12] you can visit us on June 2 and 3. If you can, we shall send you a transportation advance and make[13] a reservation for your overnight hotel accommodation in the vicinity of our St. Louis[14] office. Sincerely yours,

P. S. The enclosed pamphlet has just come from the printer and supersedes the descriptive[15] brochure that Mr. Johnson gave you. (307)

75▶ To: All Department Heads, Subject: Conference on Women in Positions of Leadership.

The enclosed advertisement of a one-day Saturday conference on Women in Positions of Leadership[1] will be of interest to all of you.

By unanimous vote the administrative committee has authorized[2] me to tell you that National Products will pay the $10 registration fee for any women employees[3] wishing to attend if their salaries are $6,500 and their job titles are in[4] a supervisory or management category. We should encourage participation of women whom[5] we label promotable; otherwise, they might feel that they are neglected in our management development[6] program. The actual and the psychological benefit of such a gesture will be worthwhile.

Please circularize[7] your eligible employees, and let me know by Monday, October 2, how many reservations to[8] make for your department. (168)

LESSON 17

76▸ To: All Supervisors, Subject: Employee Motivation.

Key supervisory personnel are being asked to attend a six-session course on Employee Motivation.[1] The course will be given from 11 a.m. to 12:30 each Thursday, beginning November 19. Because[2] of its convenient location, the third-floor conference room will be used for each class session. An informal[3] luncheon, following each session, will be served in the executive dining room.

To inaugurate the program,[4] Phil Meade, of Intercontinental Chemical Company, will discuss "Induction of New Employees." Mr. Meade[5] has developed one of the best-known induction programs in the country and is fre-

quently asked to describe it at[6] professional meetings. For the second session, we will have Professor Millard Newsome, from the graduate school[7] of Business Administration at Central University, an authority on personnel management.[8] His topic will be "After Induction, Then What?" The third session will feature Marlene Earl, of Eastland Trust Company.[9] Her subject will be "Performance Rating as a Motivation Device."

The last three sessions will be devoted[10] to improvement of motivation of employees within National Products. Supervisors will not[11] be asked to make formal presentations, but they will be expected to participate in the sessions. The fourth[12] and fifth sessions will revolve around case problems. The final session has been set aside for specific recommendations[13] for improvement of our personnel policies and practices.

Because we want a maximum amount[14] of pooling and sharing of ideas, we are providing each supervisor with Professor Newsome's popular[15] textbook, "Dynamic Personnel Practices." Please read this book before November 19. A suggested[16] list of books, pamphlets, and magazines pertinent to the topic is enclosed.

As you can see, National Products[17] is again offering key employees an unusual opportunity for professional development.[18] We are optimistic about your making the most of it. (372)

77▸ Miss Marie Fitzgerald, 114

East 177 Street, University City, Missouri 63565.

Dear Miss Fitzgerald: This will confirm our discussion in which I indicated that your services with NATIONAL[1] PRODUCTS will be terminated at the end of your six-month probationary period, Friday, March 8.[2] This decision is based on four considerations:

1. Your attendance has been irregular. It is interesting[3] to note that 9 of your 12 absences have been on Monday.

2. You have been late 13 times during your[4] probation.

3. You misspell many words with which every capable stenographer should be familiar.

4.[5] Your supervisor rates your work as mediocre and indicates that it has not shown noticeable improvement[6] during the six months you have been employed.

I am very sorry, Miss Fitzgerald, that it is necessary[7] to write this letter. The reasons for which you have been judged unacceptable for permanent employment with NATIONAL[8] PRODUCTS have been summarized for you in the hope that they will help you reassess your understanding of[9] procedures and practices that prevail in business offices. Sincerely yours, (194)

78▶ Professor Nathan Stern, Department of Economics, University of Arizona, Tucson, Arizona 85721.

Dear Professor Stern: As you know, Mr. Arthur Johnson was recruiting on your campus last week. He was very[1] sorry that you were away at the time of his visit and that he could not talk with you about a student in[2] whom we are very much interested.

We are considering Robert Robinson for a position in the[3] International Sales Division of NATIONAL PRODUCTS. We should like your candid evaluation of this[4] candidate. Naturally, we are screening more carefully than we would for a domestic position; therefore,[5] please be wholly frank with us.

We are particularly interested in your estimate of his understanding[6] of foreign trade and of his potential for growth. We also want to know whether you think he would be happy[7] if he were separated from his family and friends.

Any information you can give us will be regarded[8] as confidential, of course. Cordially yours, (169)

79▶ Dr. Lawrence Peters, Director of Business Education, Oak Park Public Schools, Oak Park, Illinois 60309.

Dear Doctor Peters: I am delighted to tell you that we shall be able to take five cooperative[1] work-experience students from the office-training program at Oak Park High School this September.

We prefer that they[2] work in the afternoons every school day from one o'clock until five o'clock rather than full time during[3] alternate weeks.

We were happy with the stu-

31

dents you sent us last year both as to attendance and performance. Let us[4] hope that this year's crop turns out as well. Sincerely yours, (89)

LESSON 18

80▶ Confidential, To: Harold C. Poling, Credit Manager, Subject: Helen Harris, Administrative Assistant.

Helen Harris has been with National Products for fifteen years. For the past eight years she has been assigned to John[1] Miller, sales manager, and worked closely with him until his death six months ago. Mr. Miller rated her work[2] superior; moreover, he gave her a great deal of responsibility.

As you know, Ralph Akin has now been[3] made sales manager. Of course, he is a young man whose promotions within the company have come rapidly. Miss[4] Harris remembers him as a young, inexperienced salesman who started to work here only five years ago.[5] Mr. Akin, on the other hand, is uncomfortable under the critical eye of Miss Harris, who expects[6] him to operate exactly as Mr. Miller did. He is sometimes short with her, and her reaction is[7] one of resentment.

I wonder, Harold, whether you would consider exchanging secretaries with Ralph. Your[8] secretary, Miss Williams, would work with him and Miss Harris would come to you. Miss Williams has been with the company[9] only two years; she is young and perhaps better suited temperamentally to work with Ralph. Certain advantages[10] would accrue to you. Miss Harris has always received the highest possible merit ratings. You know Miss Harris[11] personally, and she admires you greatly. I believe that you may actually be happier with[12] her than with your present secretary.

Will you consider the merits of this situation, Harold, and then[13] let me know whether you would consent to the change. When you are ready, let's discuss it over lunch. (277)

81▶ To: Section Managers, Subject: Requisitions for New Employees.

As you know, the new budget has been adopted. You also know how many new employees have been allotted[1] to your sections. It is now necessary to proceed with plans for hiring authorized new personnel. Before[2] this can be done, however, I shall need a great deal of information from each of you. You can help me to fill your[3] personnel requisitions by answering the following questions:

1. What changes do you recommend in job[4] titles? Why?

2. What changes do you recommend in job specifications for clerical workers? With the automation[5] of many office routines, we may need to reconsider such things as the educational level[6] of new employees, the kind and level of skills needed in our clerical positions, and the ap-

32

propriate[7] scores on entrance tests. Should we include a test in computer aptitude in some of the job specifications?[8] In which ones?

3. Do you recommend changes in job specifications for new employees above the[9] clerical level? For the managerial jobs allotted to your department, to what extent do you want the[10] Personnel Department to consider candidates' scholastic records? In general, do you prefer business[11] administration graduates, or do you prefer liberal arts graduates with strong emphasis on mathematics[12] and economics? Should we employ graduates of four-year programs, or should we aim for candidates with[13] a year ·of graduate training? Do you want to include work experience as a job specification, or[14] should we expect to get most of our management trainees directly out of college? What do you think of the potential[15] of the junior college graduates we have employed during the past five years? What suggestions do you have[16] for better liaison with the colleges? In my opinion, recruitment is increasingly competitive,[17] with large corporations vying with each other for the outstanding graduates each year.

4. What recommendations[18] have you for new employment tests by which candidates for either the old or the new positions in your[19] department may be screened? What recommendations have you for the modification of present tests or the adoption[20] of new tests to supersede any tests currently in use?

I should like to arrange a conference in[21] order to discuss any recommendations you may have. Let's try to reserve the morning of April 17[22] for this purpose. (443)

82▶ Mr. Peter M. Hall, 4201 Sixteenth Street, Chicago, Illinois 60624.

Dear Mr. Hall: Subject: Your Social Security Number. Our Payroll Department reports that you gave them a[1] social security number that differs from the one contained in your employment credential on file in this[2] office.

Will you please check your official record and give me the correct number. Sincerely yours, (57)

LESSON 19

87▶ To: Miss Alice Evans, Supervisor of In-Service Training, Subject: Education Program.

In compliance with your request, I am submitting to you, as chairman of the all-company education[1] committee, my concept of the various facets of a progressive program.

1. Training to upgrade clerical[2] skills should be given within the company. Employees who complete relevant courses at outside institutions[3] should be reimbursed for their tuition.

2. Employees selected for supervisory training should[4] take courses inside the company on company time. Those who are

approved for such training and who complete courses[5] in supervision at the university level should be reimbursed for their tuition.

3. An expanded[6] executive training program should be developed. Each year three promising young executives should be[7] sent to postgraduate schools of business administration for one semester. All executives should be urged[8] to attend appropriate management seminars and discussion groups; the company should pay the admission[9] fees.

4. All employees should be encouraged to join professional organizations in order to broaden[10] their understanding of their field of work. It is recommended that National Products pay membership dues and[11] expenses for meals. Such expense could suitably be charged to the education budget. (236)

88▶ Mr. Henry Bell, Bell Industries, El Paso, Texas 79906.

Dear Mr. Bell: At the request of Harold Bronson, 28 Iowa Street, El Paso, Texas, I am writing[1] you this letter to verify his record of employment with NATIONAL PRODUCTS for three years, from June 1,[2] 1963, to May 31, 1966.

During that period his chief assignment was in[3] the field of labor relations, where he handled most of the employee grievances. We enjoyed an unusually[4] peaceful three years, largely because of his skill in maintaining such good liaison with our employees at[5] both the

management and worker levels. He had the reputation of being not only fair but also[6] courageous and unyielding when a decision had to be enforced.

During the time he was with us, he regularly[7] enrolled for graduate courses in his field at Central University. He was popular as a[8] speaker on labor relations in this vicinity and has written a pamphlet on the subject.

He also[9] performed miscellaneous duties in the personnel field when he was with us, and his performance was superior[10] in all aspects. He understands interviewing techniques, employee testing, induction, and evaluation.[11] Judging from his performance with us for three years, I would say that he would bring creativity and[12] initiative to your company. I envy you in being able to hire Mr. Bronson. It is unfortunate[13] for us that his health forced him to move from this vicinity. Sincerely yours, (275)

89▶ To: Miss Nancy Watson, Office Services, Subject: Tuition Refund.

I have your application for a tuition refund of $60 for a course in French that you have just[1] completed at City College. Unfortunately, this request must be denied.

If you will review page 8 of[2] our pamphlet, Your Educational Growth at National, you will see that "only courses that improve your performance[3] on the job are eligible for reimbursement." Undoubtedly, a course in

French improves your educational[4] background; nevertheless, it cannot be considered job-related in the sense that is intended.

The[5] enclosed list of City College courses in secretarial studies, economics, and business administration[6] may give you direction in choosing additional courses. (133)

* * *

▶ Make a shorthand list of brief outlines of words related to your business. Use the intersecting principle. This is particularly helpful for the new worker.

LESSON 20

91▶ Memo to All Employees, Subject: Major Medical Insurance.

You will be glad to know that your company is interested in making available to all employees[1] and their immediate families an option to purchase major medical protection up to $20,000.[2] The company will pay 60 percent of the premiums for this fringe benefit, and each insured employee[3] will pay only 40 percent. A complete description of the proposed plan and rate cards for your payroll deductions,[4] if you elect the plan, are enclosed.

This insurance may be carried in addition to your Blue Cross and Blue[5] Shield coverage for normal hospitalization and medical services.

It will be possible to obtain[6] major medical protection only if at least half of our employees sign for it. Therefore, please study the[7] enclosed description of the benefits carefully; then complete the enclosed application and return it to[8] Miss Alice Brown. (163)

92▶ To: All Employees, Subject: Suggestion System.

Every employee is eligible for cash awards for any of his suggestions for improving National[1] Products that are accepted. Suggestions may be presented for more efficient operation of[2] equipment, for changes in systems or procedures that result in a better flow of work, for ways of reducing[3] expenses, for simplified direction of traffic from plant to customer, for improved design and control[4] of forms, for handling grievances, for stimulation of employee initiative, and for better manufacturing[5] techniques.

Your suggestions will be carefully considered by a Suggestions Committee established[6] just for that purpose. If your idea should be accepted, you will receive a cash award based on the estimated[7] savings to the company. These awards are not token payments. In one case, for instance, an assembly-line[8] worker was paid $1,000 for a suggestion that completely eliminated one step in[9] manufacturing our water gauges. Another award was given to a clerical worker who suggested[10] a new method of distributing reports that eliminated the need for two copies. This recommendation[11] saved an estimated $50 a month in office time.

The cash value of a suggestion that is [12] adopted is important, of course; but of greater significance than the money is the fact that the employee [13] has identified himself as a worker with initiative and creativity, an employee [14] to be considered favorably for the next promotion.

There is a suggestion box near the elevator [15] on each floor. Attached to the box are blank forms for use in submitting your suggestions. Submit as many suggestions [16] as you wish, but use a separate form for each one. Every blank is numbered, and a detachable stub is [17] stamped with the same number. Just tear off the stub and keep it. Because your Suggestions Committee does not know the person [18] submitting a suggestion, it must consider each entry solely on its merits.

The person performing [19] the job is the one best qualified to propose innovations. Start now to analyze your job, and think about [20] how you might increase your productivity. An idea that sounds familiar to you may have been overlooked [21] by your supervisor.

Send it today; tomorrow could be too late. (433)

Unit 5

Secretarial Assignment

1 The accompanying catalog warrants the stockholders' attention.

2 The tentative date of the premiere is all right with me.

3 This extraordinary biographical note appears in Miller's new volume of literary criticism.

4 Administrative difficulties in planning stockholders' meetings are inevitable.

5 The accompanying advertisement will appear in the column adjacent to the review.

6 The old building adjacent to ours is being dismantled.

7 Do her achievements warrant her inclusion in a volume identifying outstanding businesswomen?

8 A club sponsor should be accessible to the Administrative Committee.

9 Phenomenal achievements sometimes invite unwarranted criticism.

10 Publication of the biographical volume is tentatively set for May 1.

LESSON 21

1 The workers received an hour's time off at their boss's request.

2 The people's choice is reflected at the polls.

3 A minute's delay often means the difference between life and death.

4 The sons-in-law's reaction to their mother-in-law's will was inevitable.

5 Our willingness to buy the buildings depends on the three owners' prices.

6 The installation of the senators-elect occurs in January.

7 Smith's grocery will be closed

until the company's labor negotiations are completed.

8 Women's rights were discussed in the article in the Reader's Digest.

9 Our class's reunion will be held at Ross's Restaurant.

10 Public interest was aroused when the six firms' cooperation was announced.

93▶ Mr. Herbert Miller, Miller's Grocery, Bluefield, West Virginia 24701.

Dear Mr. Miller: I understand that you are handling the publicity for the West Virginia State Retailers[1] Association's meeting in Charleston on Friday, April 17. Since Mr. Henry M. Simpson, the[2] president of NATIONAL PRODUCTS, is the keynote speaker, I am sure you will want to feature his address in[3] your state magazine and in the newspapers throughout West Virginia.

I am enclosing a preliminary[4] copy of Mr. Simpson's speech to assist you in preparing your release. Knowing the limited budget of[5] most organizations, NATIONAL PRODUCTS is arranging for Reynolds Photographers to take pictures of Mr.[6] Simpson delivering his address. By 1 p.m. of April 17 you will have 25 glossy prints[7] that can be rushed to newspapers in time for the evening editions. I suggest that the news story precede them[8] by at least one day.

All that we ask is that you identify Mr. Simpson as president of NATIONAL[9] PRODUCTS, INC., St. Louis, Missouri, in all publicity. You need not send us copies of any[10] publicity resulting from your story and the pictures; our clipping service will supply us. Yours very[11] truly, (221)

94▶ Reynolds Photographers, 714 South Lewis Street, Charleston, West Virginia 25302.

Gentlemen: Mr. Henry M. Simpson, president of NATIONAL PRODUCTS, INC., will be the principal[1] speaker at the West Virginia State Retailers Association during its annual meeting[2] on Friday, April 17. He is scheduled to make his presentation at 10 a.m.

We should like you to take[3] pictures from which you will make 25 glossy prints suitable for reproduction in the official magazine[4] of the organization and in newspapers throughout West Virginia. Please show Mr. Simpson actually[5] giving his speech or with the officers of the association on the dais.

Be sure that the identifying[6] caption on the back of each print includes the words, "President of NATIONAL PRODUCTS, INC.,[7] St. Louis, Missouri." Please have the prints available for distribution by 1 p.m. so that they will make[8] the evening editions.

The prints are to be delivered to Herbert Miller in the pressroom of the Continental[9] Hotel. As you can see from the enclosed letter, Mr. Miller will be expecting these prints by 1 p.m.[10]

Please mark the bill for these prints for my attention, and send it to the address given on the letterhead. Sincerely[11] yours, (221)

95▶ The Wall Street Journal, Wall Street, New York, New York 10005.

Gentlemen: The earnings report of NATIONAL PRODUCTS, INC., for the quarter ending June 30[1] is enclosed.

You will note that sales increased $125,000, or 8 percent, and that earnings[2] increased from $.96 to $1.08, or 12½ percent, over the same quarter last year.

Although[3] we know that you will publish the summary report, we are hoping that this rather phenomenal growth will[4] warrant a separate story. Sincerely yours, (89)

96▶ Professor Mildred Adamson, Northern State Teachers College, Duluth, Minnesota 55805.

Dear Professor Adamson: Here is the glossy print of the illustration that you recently sent us, along[1] with a request for permission to use it in your forthcoming book, "Being An Efficient Secretary."

We[2] are glad to give you this permission. All that we ask is that you call the editor-in-chief's attention to our[3] request for a credit line. It should read: Courtesy of NATIONAL PRODUCTS, INC., St. Louis, Missouri.[4] We should appreciate a copy of the book when it is published.

Best wishes to you in this important[5] undertaking. Sincerely yours, (104)

97▶ Professor Lawrence Wilkins, Department of Business Administration, Business Institute, Sedalia, Missouri 65303.

Dear Professor Wilkins: Would you like to have admission tickets again this year so that your students may attend[1] our annual stockholders' meeting? It will be held in the auditorium of NATIONAL PRODUCTS on Friday,[2] April 17, starting promptly at 11 a.m. We anticipate that the meeting will be over[3] by 1:30 p.m. As our building is adjacent to the bus station, it will be easily accessible[4] to your students.

Last year you requested 75 tickets. This year, because of limited space and[5] a greater interest of the public in securities, we shall have to limit the number to 50.[6] Because of the probable congestion, will you please advise your students to use the balcony seats if they wish to[7] enter and exit during the proceedings.

Would it be advantageous, Professor Wilkins, if we sent you copies[8] of our annual report, which describes NATIONAL PRODUCTS' phenomenal growth? Perhaps these copies could be[9] the basis of discussion in the classroom prior to the stockholders' meeting. If they would not serve a useful[10] purpose, however, we prefer not to send them, for the supply is limited.

Please let me know promptly whether[11] you can use the 50

tickets and the copies of our annual report. Your students will receive the same kit[12] of our company's new products that is given to others in attendance. Sincerely yours, (257)

98▶ To: Henry M. Simpson, President, Subject: Published Stockholders' Comments.

A new kind of corporation report is being used for the enlightenment of our stockholders. It is a[1] transcript of stockholders' comments made during the discussion period following the main business of the annual[2] meeting. After studying 15 such printed reports during the past two months, all in dialogue form,[3] I recommend that we print a transcript of the stockholders' questions and the responses of our corporate officials.[4] The report would be mailed to every stockholder, to members of the press, and to financial analysts[5] as a matter of public information.

The advantages are:
1. Stockholders would feel closer to the[6] company in which they own shares if they feel that their questions are welcome and will be answered. Although only a[7] relatively small number of stockholders attend the annual meeting, those not in attendance would be drawn[8] closer to the company by this report.
2. Stockholders would feel that management is interested in them[9] and wants to help them understand how their company is operated. If they could get verbatim answers to[10] questions, made by corporation offi-

cials, they would have more confidence in the company's leadership.
3. Inasmuch[11] as questions being asked from the floor are the ones most stockholders want answered, this transcript would summarize[12] the portion of the proceedings that deal with stockholders' interests.

The disadvantage is:
Some of the stockholders[13] attending the annual meetings are minority owners who make a profession of attending these[14] sessions for the purpose of heckling the management. They are not typical of the majority, who are[15] objectively motivated. Frequently they represent a women's shareholder organization that is well[16] known for its loquacious leadership. With this in mind, it might be necessary to edit both the questions and[17] the answers.

A preliminary cost estimate for 1,500 copies of an 8-page, 6-by-9-inch[18] booklet is $500. If you agree with me, Mr. Simpson, that a report of this kind would strengthen[19] our public information program, you may wish to discuss it with the administrative committee at[20] its next meeting. It will be necessary to start planning the report almost immediately if it is[21] authorized. (421)

99▶ Mr. John R. McCann, Editorial Office, Fortune Magazine, Time & Life Building, Avenue of the Americas at 50th Street, New York, New York 10019.

Dear Mr. McCann: I am sending you today, in a separate

package by registered, insured mail,[1] materials for research on your feature article on the growth of NATIONAL PRODUCTS.

We are so pleased that you[2] are going to publish the story that we want to do everything possible to simplify your preparation[3] of it.

You will have access to additional material housed in our business archives when you visit[4] NATIONAL PRODUCTS headquarters.

Let me know when you plan to come so that I can set up appointments with the[5] company officials whom you designate. Sincerely yours, (111)

LESSON 23

100▶ Press Release, For Release: April 3.

EDUCATIONAL GIFTS AT NATIONAL PRODUCTS

NATIONAL PRODUCTS, INC., St. Louis, Missouri, has just announced gifts of $100,000[1] to higher education for the coming year. The bulk of the money, $50,000, will be given[2] to Missouri Institute of Technology.

Mr. Henry M. Simpson, president, said, "We are especially[3] interested in Missouri Tech because it provides advanced courses taken by at least 25[4] men in Research and Development here at NATIONAL PRODUCTS every year."

Washington University[5] received $25,000 for its school of business. The other $25,000 was allocated[6] as follows: $10,000 to Central College; $10,000 to Park College; and $5,000[7] to Westminster College. All three of the small institutions are liberal arts colleges. NATIONAL PRODUCTS[8] regularly recruits graduates from these colleges for employment in its St. Louis headquarters.

In addition[9] to these grants, NATIONAL PRODUCTS pays one-half of four years' tuition for a son or daughter of any[10] employee earning less than $15,000 a year. The child, however, must maintain a C average[11] to qualify for company scholarships. To date, 38 children have been graduated from college under[12] this employees' benefit plan. (247)

101▶ Press Release to St. Louis Newspapers.

COMMUNITY CHEST CHAIRMAN

Henry Walters, vice-president of NATIONAL PRODUCTS, INC., of St. Louis, was named chairman of[1] the St. Louis Community Chest at a meeting of the board of directors at the Chase Hotel on Wednesday,[2] October 22. Mr. Walters was vice-chairman of the campaign last year.

This year's goal is $10,000,-000.[3] Subscriptions to the Community Chest are divided among 26 carefully chosen charities.[4] In this way citizens can make one contribution, and multiple solicitations are reduced. It is[5] possible, however, to earmark any contribution for a specific fund if the donor wishes to do[6] so.

Mr. Walters said, "I am sure

that the people of St. Louis will open their hearts to community needs[7] and will pledge generously for the unfortunate among us. I intend to open the campaign for business[8] gifts in my own organization, NATIONAL PRODUCTS. I am sure that we can set the pattern of giving for[9] the entire community."

Mr. Harold Horton, treasurer of The Fair, will assist Mr. Walters as vice-chairman.[10] Mrs. Helen Woods, secretary of the Suburban Insurance Company, will head the women's division[11] of the campaign. (224)

102▶ To: Vincent M. Regan, Research and Development, Subject: Project 72.

Your demonstration of Project 72 to key personnel over closed-circuit television on Thursday[1] was most impressive. The presentation by the Advertising Department of preliminary plans for[2] launching the new product next year also was excellent. Of course, many changes will be made before final[3] approval of both the product and the advertising will be given.

The importance of security measures[4] to prevent our company's leaking any technical information cannot be emphasized too much. However,[5] it might be advantageous to release from time to time during the year some short statements about the product's[6] successful testings. In this way we can create an interest in it and thus obtain an audience watching[7] for its appearance. These news notes would appear in such

publications as Business Week or Nation's Business and in[8] the business pages of the newspapers in such columns as "Business in Brief."

I am sending a copy of this[9] letter to Mr. Simpson for his consideration. The Administrative Committee would, of course, have to[10] approve the plan; but this preliminary exploration of the idea with you may lead you to support such[11] a proposal and to supply information about final tests and suggestions appropriate for public[12] information. If the idea is approved, I would depend on you for the background information for the[13] releases. (261)

103▶ To: Mr. Henry M. Simpson, President, Subject: Project 72.

The enclosed letter is self-explanatory. You may feel that security is more important than preliminary[1] interest. If so, I shall understand your point of view. (33)

LESSON 24

108▶ To: Helene Marie Potter, Assistant, Public Information Service, Subject: International Trade Show.

This will confirm our telephone conversation this morning, at which time you were asked to take charge of our product[1] booth at the International Trade show, which is to be held at the Coliseum in New York from October[2] 3 to 6. Because this type of assignment is new to you, I want to give you several suggestions that may[3] help you to avoid some of the pitfalls I encountered in carrying out this assignment for five years.

1. Your[4] budget for rental, materials, transportation, and labor charges for setting up and tearing down the display[5] is $2,500. This figure does not, of course, include operating salaries, as the booth[6] will be manned by regular sales employees.

Be sure to stay within this budget! One of the easiest ways to[7] get in trouble with management is to run out of money and then find you must request a budget supplement.[8]

2. You will employ union labor in moving the exhibit in and out of the Coliseum. Union[9] laborers charge time and a half after five o'clock and on weekends. Fortunately, the show starts on Tuesday and ends[10] on Thursday. You can avoid extra costs if you go in on Monday afternoon and schedule your workmen to finish[11] before five o'clock. You should begin dismantling the exhibit early Friday morning, as you are required[12] to release your space by noon for the next Coliseum event. When you unpack, save all boxes for repacking[13] the exhibit.

3. Be sure to ship your materials early enough to have them available by noon on[14] Monday. Try to allow for all those crises that seem inevitable when a number of boxes are shipped.

4.[15] Make a typewritten schedule of the hours during which each salesman will attend the booth. Post it and follow it[16] rigidly. You may expect full cooperation from our New York sales personnel, but even the most reliable[17] employee must be held to a schedule.

I should like to see your scale model of the exhibit when it is[18] completed. Please call on me for any additional guidance you may need. (374)

109▶ Mr. Phillip L. Stanwood, Midwestern District Manager, National Products, Inc., 2211 Front Street, Houston, Texas 77017.

Dear Phil: Please arrange to send me several different glossy photographs of the new Houston plant for inclusion[1] in this year's annual report. We plan to use color for this issue; so ask your photographer to give[2] us several pictures of the building and landscaping.

Do you have good shots of the ceremonies on opening[3] day? If any dignitaries attended, such as the Governor, senators, or major city officials,[4] it would be effective to show them greeting you and Henry Simpson.

Do you have pictures that show the products[5] we manufacture or some distinctive operation of this new installation? Your judgment will suffice, Phil,[6] for you are thoroughly familiar with the whole operation and can pinpoint the things that should be emphasized.[7]

In addition, I should appreciate it if you would take a hard look at last year's annual report and then[8] send me your suggestions on how it can be approved. Your suggestions are always helpful; I have learned to rely[9] upon them. Sincerely yours, (184)

* * *

▶ If you take dictation from more than one person, it is best to keep a separate notebook for each dictator. If this is not possible, be sure to note the initials of the dictator at the beginning of each letter.

LESSON 25

111▶ To: All Company Officers, Subject: Biographical Data and Photographs.

Our Public Information Service frequently needs biographical data about company officials[1] on very short notice. In order to have up-to-date information, we are asking you to complete the enclosed[2] questionnaire and return it by Monday, June 3.

We are also concerned about the ancient photographs on[3] file for many of our officers. If you have not had a picture taken within the last five years, please make arrangements[4] with our photographer. (86)

112▶ Mr. Richard C. Barry, Central College, Fairfield, Iowa 52556.

Dear Mr. Barry: Your letter of June 8 requesting a short history of our company and a copy[1] of

the organization chart for the entire corporation as well as for the headquarters offices has[2] been referred to me.

We appreciate your interest in our company and are happy to send you all the[3] material we have available for use in your term paper. Under separate cover we are sending[4] you the history, a catalog describing the products that we manufacture, a pamphlet called "You at[5] National Products," and the organization chart for the corporation.

I regret, however, that we do not[6] have a copy of the organization chart for the headquarters offices. This chart is now in the process[7] of revision and will probably not be available before the end of the college year.

If there is any[8] other information that you would like to have, please let me know. We are always glad to cooperate with[9] college students in their search for current business information. Cordially yours, (194)

113▶ Mr. Jack M. Roche, Room 1679Y, State Department, Washington, D. C. 20002.

Dear Mr. Roche: Your letter to Mr. Henry M. Simpson, president of NATIONAL PRODUCTS, INC.,[1] has been turned over to me for handling.

As he told you, we are delighted that you thought of our company[2] in connection with the visit of 15 Japanese businessmen to various representative corporations[3] in the United States. As we are in the process of negotiating for wider distribution[4] of our products in

Japan, we consider this an extraordinary opportunity to tell the story[5] of our company.

The date you suggest, September 10, is all right with us. We should like to plan a full day's[6] activities here in our principal factory and in our headquarters. Can you plan to arrive with your party[7] by 9:30?

After a welcoming speech by our president, our vice-president in charge of research and development[8] can describe the principal products that we manufacture. Then our factory manager can discuss[9] our manufacturing methods. After these two presentations, we shall all be ready for lunch. As we are in[10] a suburban location, I think it would be best for us to have a short luncheon period and eat in the[11] executive dining room. After lunch perhaps we can show the film "Our National Story," which has just been[12] developed for our annual stockholders' meeting. The final talk would be given by our vice-president in charge[13] of marketing.

NATIONAL PRODUCTS would like to entertain all our visitors for dinner at the St. Louis[14] Athletic Club. All company officers would also be invited.

Please feel free to give any criticism[15] you wish of these tentative plans. You are more familiar with the objectives of this international program[16] than we are, and you also know how other companies are arranging their schedules. We shall appreciate[17] your suggestions. Sincerely yours, (345)

Unit 6

Secretarial Assignment

1 The acquisition of negotiable bonds enables us to finance the project.
2 The auditors questioned our procedure for amortizing the debt.
3 Do you recommend municipal debenture bonds?
4 The $450,000 deficit places their company in a dilemma.
5 The intricacies of investment procedures appeal to a financier.
6 The agenda includes discussion of diversification of operations.
7 Auditors made comparative studies of expense vouchers for two fiscal years.
8 We mailed withholding tax statements for the fiscal year.
9 He signed a negotiable note for the new equipment.
10 Lowering the tariff will favor acquisition of foreign markets.
11 The ratio of stocks to bonds in a financier's portfolio is important.

LESSON 26

1 We employ 125 clerks in eight departments.
2 Thirty-five years ago this headquarters site was a cornfield.
3 The price will be increased $3 a dozen after six months.
4 We borrowed the money at 5 percent, a 1 percent increase over the old rate.
5 Put the information on 3- by

5-inch cards.

6 October 15, 1912, is the date of his birth.

7 The note is due on the 15th of November.

8 Almost a thousand inquiries a week come into our office.

9 I found over two hundred citations for my report.

10 Do you say "5 p.m." or "five o'clock"?

11 I found 31 exceptions to the general rule.

12 He bought Wabash at 103 last week.

13 He has one chance in a hundred of getting the job.

14 We made delivery to 416 Fourth Street.

15 We had a 6 percent decrease in profits last year.

16 There were almost a thousand people outside the theater.

114▶ To: Glenn C. Hunter, Chief Auditor, Subject: Audit for District Offices.

Dear Glenn: Have you planned the annual audit for our district offices? I think it would be a good idea[1] to alter the schedule this year so that the district managers won't know when to expect the auditors. This is[2] standard procedure in many companies, and I'm told it works well.

Wouldn't it be advisable to hold a[3] training session with the auditors before they go into the field? At that time you could present a specimen[4] audit and explain any new tax regulations that should be considered in this year's audit. As you know, more[5] careful scrutiny of expense account reports should

be made. The auditors should also examine supporting[6] vouchers carefully. A spot check on inventory should be sufficient as long as we maintain our computer[7] control that updates inventory information weekly.

I know, Glenn, that this year's audit will represent your[8] usual efficient performance. If there is any way in which I can help you in organizing it, let[9] me know. Please bring your preliminary plans with you when you come to my office next week. We can discuss them then.[10] Cordially yours, (202)

115▶ To: William A. Scanlon, Payroll, Subject: Withholding Tax Statement.

If we spread the preparation of withholding tax statements over a six-week period and thus avoid a[1] peak work load, don't you think we can do this job without hiring additional personnel? Although there are 385[2] employees in the St. Louis headquarters, the present staff could do the work if given sufficient[3] time.

I suggest that we start the work on January 15 and spread it through January and February.[4] We should not mail the statements, however, until March 1 so that last-minute corrections can be made for any[5] changes occurring between January 15 and February 28.

Although some employees begin[6] asking for these forms before February 1 so that they may compute their income taxes and submit their[7] returns early, a March 1 report is much more accurate and should be adopted.

Writing the February[8] checks can be facilitated if the payroll is made up one week early for this critical period.[9] If you agree, notices should be sent to all department heads requesting that they submit the February[10] payroll by February 15.

Please let me know whether you concur in these suggestions and will be able[11] to implement them. (223)

116▶ To: Mr. Henry M. Simpson, President, Subject: Inventory Levels.

While our sales have risen 6 percent during the past year, our purchases have not risen proportionately,[1] making it difficut to maintain former inventory levels. The depletion of inventories has not reached[2] alarming heights. Although computerized inventory control and faster transportation enable us to[3] reduce our stocks by 3 percent without harmful effects, we have now gone below that figure.

Difficulty in[4] negotiating the new labor contracts could lead to strikes, and the unsettled condition of the transportation[5] industry could have a disastrous effect on the supply of raw materials unless we raise our[6] inventories appreciably. Another factor favoring higher inventories is the possibility[7] of increased prices for raw materials if the inflationary trend continues.

For these reasons, Mr.[8] Simpson, I recommend that this problem be placed on the agenda of the Administrative Committee at[9] its next meeting. (183)

* * *

▶ If your boss constantly forgets to tell you about unexpected engagements and you frequently have no idea where he has gone, work out a reminder system. You might keep a notebook in a certain place on his desk. Large lettering at the top of each page could read something like this: "I have gone to........." "Will be back at ...."

LESSON 27

117▶ To: Henry M. Simpson, Chairman Administrative Committee, Subject: Production Ratios.

This information is sent in answer to your request of September 3 for data about unit labor[1] costs in the regional distribution centers of National Products.

During the past twelve months (August 31[2] of last year to September 1 of this year), we negotiated a 3 percent wage increase for all[3] production workers across the board. This increase will remain in effect until August 31 of next year, at[4] which time this labor contract expires. During the same fiscal period, however, we increased man-hour production[5] by 3 percent.

Clerical and administrative salaries rose sharply during the same period. This[6] additional overhead had a depressing effect on net operating profits. However, with production[7] labor costs stabilized for the next twelve months, we should be able to hold the "profit line." I believe increased[8] production will offset all wage increases. (168)

118▶ To: Lawrence F. Markham, Traffic Manager, Subject: Comparison of Methods of Shipping.

Please prepare a report on sending a 20-pound and a 150-pound shipment to each of our six[1] distribution centers by each of the following methods of transportation: truck, railroad, and airfreight. Include[2] comparative figures on cost of shipping, cost of packing (if the cost varies by type of transportation), and[3] the length of time required for delivery to each center. Don't guess on delivery time; actually check[4] it out on recent shipments.

What present policies determine the method of shipment used for various types[5] of merchandise? Do you have recommendations for any changes?

At a meeting I attended recently,[6] the speaker indicated that more and more corporations are able to reduce inventories, and thus tie[7] up less cash, by using airfreight regularly rather than only in emergencies. We should investigate[8] this trend.

Can you have the report ready for me by November 7? (173)

119▶ To: Mr. Henry M. Simpson, President, Subject: Long-Term Financing of Proposed New Factory.

My recommendation for long-term financing of the proposed new factory is that we issue callable[1] 2½ percent bonds for $750,000 on January 1 of next year. These[2] would be 20-year bonds, but we would plan to call the issue before maturity if we can amortize the[3] debt sooner. I suggest that we set up an amortization fund next year for this purpose; and if profits[4] actually materialize as expected, we can retire the bonds at the end of ten years.

I have discussed[5] the problem with Edward Barnes, our industrial counselor at the Second National Bank; he recommended[6] the plan outlined here. The Second National Bank would assist us in securing the underwriter of the issue,[7] but I assume that Wilson and Smith would undertake this responsibility, as they have done in the past.[8]

Please tell me what steps you wish me to take next. (168)

120▶ Bank of Commerce, 410 Lake Avenue, Chicago, Illinois 60612.

Gentlemen: Your advertisement in the July issue of Fortune was read with interest by a number of NATIONAL[1] PRODUCTS people. We have always bought our major equipment; but your plan of purchasing equipment and leasing[2] it to industrial organizations — everything from bulldozers to typewriters, including computers,[3] electronic equipment, plant equipment, construction equipment, and machine tools — is appealing. You state[4] that we can draw up the specifications and that you will buy what we request. You also state that you will lease[5] over fixed terms at negotiable costs.

If such an arrangement would free our working capital for other purposes,[6] we should like to investigate the new concept thoroughly. We know of no such offer from local banks;[7] so we may wish to deal with a bank in a neighboring city.

Enclosed is our current annual report. It[8] describes our corporation and will give you an opportunity to see that our operations are extensive[9] and that we are in an enviable financial position.

Please send us complete information about[10] the plan, as we are now analyzing our total equipment needs. If we decide to pursue the matter further[11] and obtain cost estimates, perhaps a meeting with your representative could be arranged. Yours very truly,[12] (240)

121▶ Mr. Herbert B. Greenwald, President, First National Bank, Balboa at Sacramento Street, San Diego, California 92116.

Dear Mr. Greenwald: NATIONAL PRODUCTS, INC., wishes to apply for a 90-day loan for[1] $50,000 for short-term financing of current operations of its new distribution center in[2] San Diego. Although capital expenditure for the construction of the plant has been covered by long-term[3] financing, we need ready cash during the next three months, during which time our product sales generally fall off[4] slightly.

Enclosed is our operating statement for your preliminary study. May I discuss this request[5] with you when I am in San Diego on Tuesday, September 19? Yours very truly, (117)

122▶ Wilson and Smith, One Wall Street, New York, New York 10005.

Gentlemen: Our Administrative Committee has authorized the issuance of callable $2\frac{1}{2}$[1] percent, 20-year debenture bonds for $750,000 on January 1, 1966,[2] for the financing of our new factory in Knoxville.

Since you have handled the sale of similar[3] bonds for us in the past, we are asking you to arrange interviews with possible underwriters.

Do you think[4] that I could plan to meet with them on Tuesday, September 2; or would that date rush you too much? Do you anticipate[5] any change in the bond market that might make it advisable to delay the sale of this issue until[6] after the election? Yours very truly, (127)

LESSON 28

123▶ To: Ralph C. Akin, Sales Manager, Subject: Car Rentals.

An examination of salesmen's expense accounts for the past year leads me to question our present practices[1] with regard to the rental of cars by salesmen for use in their territories. We have a policy of[2] permitting salesmen to rent any type of car they want, and we have exercised no control over the rental. I[3] suspect that the privilege of rental has in some cases been abused so that salesmen rent the cars for longer[4] periods than necessary and also choose higher priced cars than are required for their business needs.

The volume[5] of our car rentals has become so large that I believe we can now obtain a blanket contract for our entire[6] fleet of automobiles on a yearly basis. We could thus reduce the operating expense in the Sales[7] Department appreciably. This would mean, of course, that we could deal only with the one or two agencies operating[8] on a nationwide scale.

What is your own reaction to this proposal to explore the possibility[9] of a blanket contract? How do you think your salesmen would feel about it, especially if the contract covers[10] rental of medium-priced cars only? Should we ask their preference as to the agency chosen? Can you project[11] the company's car-rental needs for next year beginning January 1?

Will you please summarize the[12] information from the past three months' expense-account forms as to the rental agencies used and the make of automobile[13] rented.

Please bring this information to a conference with me two weeks from today. Check your calendar,[14] and then ask my secretary to select an hour when we are both free. (293)

124▶ To: Mr. Henry M. Simpson, President, Subject: November Credit Collection Report.

The enclosed report of collections for November merits study. Harry Poling has also submitted[1] comparative figures on collections in representative corporations, which I am also sending along[2] to you.

You will see that our collections are better by far than those of other companies. The percentage of[3] our customers taking their cash discounts is 2 percent higher, and the percentage paying within 30 days[4] is 3 percent higher.

You will agree, I am sure, that Mr. Poling is doing an outstanding job in keeping[5] the flow of cash from our accounts unusually high. In my opinion, he is a man in the organization[6] who has a real future ahead of him. We should keep our eyes on him for promotion. (137)

125▶ Mr. J. Alan Franklin, Vice-President, The Martin-Williamson Company, 416 Delaware Road, Baltimore, Maryland 21208.

Dear Mr. Franklin: Your company took a step two years ago that we are now considering. Would you share your[1] experience with us?

Our volume of business has grown to the point where we are eligible to apply for[2] listing on the New York Stock Exchange. As you know, we have been listed on the American

Stock Exchange for the past[3] nine years. Our Administrative Committee has asked me to make an informal report based on opinions of[4] officials in other companies that recently became listed on the "big board." What steps did you take prior[5] to filing your application with the Securities and Exchange Commission? What effect has the listing had[6] on the price of your stock? Knowing what you now know, would you make the change again?

Any guidance you can give us will[7] be very much appreciated. Yours very truly, (150)

126▶ To: Harold C. Poling, Credit Manager, Subject: Cash Flow.

Congratulations, Harold, on a job well done. Your November analysis of charge accounts indicates that your[1] collections are running well ahead of expectations. Your reduction of the average length of time an[2] account remains unpaid is a valuable contribution to the short-term financing of National Products[3] operations. Thank you for providing comparative figures on the collection schedules of other[4] corporations and ours. I already knew that our collections were unusually good, but you have enabled[5] me to see our position more clearly.

I hope that we shall be able to maintain as good a record in December.[6] Payments are always slower during a holiday season, though, and this year will probably conform to[7] the usual pattern. However, I should like to have your estimate of December collections by November[8] 20 so that I can anticipate our cash needs in time to arrange necessary financing. (178)

LESSON 29

131▶ Mr. Vincent Jones, Production Manager, National Products, Inc., 271 Mount Washington Boulevard, Louisville, Kentucky 40219.

Dear Vincent: Mr. Harold Jamison, vice-president in charge of Research and Development, and I are planning[1] a tour of six National Products installations to discuss next year's production plans. Will it be convenient for[2] you to meet with us on August 11 and 12? If so, we shall plan to include the Louisville plant in our[3] itinerary at that time. If these two days conflict with plans you have already made, we can arrange to come[4] to Louisville at the end of our trip rather than at the beginning. This change would bring us to your plant on August[5] 17 and 18.

In preparation for the conference, a great deal of information should be assembled[6] and evaluated. We need a clear picture of your operations since the Louisville plant started[7] production, especially the degree to which you have utilized space and equipment. Can you break down these figures[8] on a monthly basis?

We are very much interested

in the availability of semiskilled labor[9] in the vicinity. Any expansion of our activities in Louisville would hinge on the procurement[10] of such personnel. What is your considered judgment on this point? If you can support an opinion with facts[11] and figures, we would be grateful.

While we are in your city, I want to have a conference with the representative[12] of the Citizens National Bank, in which our funds are deposited. Would you be good enough to arrange[13] a luncheon with him at the City Club. Also, please send me a brief memorandum about him before the[14] meeting.

Let me know immediately the dates you prefer for our meetings and whether there is any way we[15] can help you prepare for our visit. We want our meetings to be as fruitful as possible. Cordially yours, (318)

132▶ Mr. Herbert Ashe, Production Manager, National Products, Inc., 2198 Lafayette Street, New Orleans, Louisiana 70113.

Dear Herb: Harold Jamison and I are touring our installations this month to discuss next year's production schedules.[1]

We should like to visit our New Orleans plant on August 12 and 13 if those dates will be convenient for[2] you.

We are assembling such production figures, procurement costs, payroll, and financial data as are available[3] from our computer center here at headquarters; however, we feel that a conference and tour of your[4]

facilities will provide supplementary information about problems peculiar to your operation.[5] We shall depend on you to prepare reports not available to us on our computer setup.

Let me[6] know if there is any additional preliminary preparation that we can make for this meeting that[7] will make it more fruitful. I can't emphasize enough the importance of our long-range planning at this conference.[8] Yours truly, (162)

133▶ Brewster & Noble, Public Accountants, 11 Wall Street, New York, New York 10005.

Gentlemen: At the annual meeting of the stockholders of NATIONAL PRODUCTS on April 9, the recommendation[1] to retain your company as our accountants for the next calendar year was approved.

Will you please[2] arrange for your attorney to meet with our attorneys, Jones and Billings, to discuss the contract. I hope that it can[3] be drawn up almost immediately so that it can be approved by our Administrative Committee at[4] its meeting on the 17th of May. Although I realize that recent legislation affects the scope of[5] an auditor's activities, I ask that the changes in the new contract be kept to a minimum. Yours truly,[6] (120)

LESSON 30

136▶ Chamber of Commerce, Houston, Texas 77031.

Gentlemen: We have been in correspondence with the Industrial Development Board of the state of Texas[1] in Austin about the desirability of locating a new plant in Texas. Its reply has encouraged[2] us to investigate Houston as a recommended site.

Will you please answer the following questions so[3] that we may continue our search for the best possible location:

1. Would we find local sources of[4] polyethylene, synthetic rubber, and plastic materials near Houston?

2. Is there an adequate industrial[5] labor force? With the huge air-space installations there, this may present a problem.

3. What is the going rate[6] of factory wages?

4. Will Texas, and especially Houston, provide a market for NATIONAL PRODUCTS?[7] What is the per capita income and educational level of residents?

5. What comparative figures[8] can you supply about freight rates?

6. Are preferential airfreight rates given to Houston manufacturers?[9]

7. What plans are under way for deepening the channel to the Galveston port?

8. Can you suggest a site[10] that would qualify us for an urban-renewal loan?

If your reply confirms our present opinions, a[11] committee from our headquarters will probably visit your city. Yours truly, (234)

137▶ Memo to Arthur Williamson, Director of Public Information, Subject: Purchase of Elmira Plant.

Congratulations, Art, on your coverage of this news story. I had expected space in the St. Louis,[1] Chicago, New York, and San Francisco papers; but getting a feature on the front page of Thursday's Wall Street Journal[2] is a real coup. I note that copy has already been accepted for this week's issue of Business Week, which is[3] now in press. Incidentally, getting coverage in this important publication is no small accomplishment.[4]

I do have a suggestion for the Fortune story. Since the announcement is scheduled for the New Products column,[5] it must be rewritten. Could you use a picture of our latest aeroseal bottle and tie into the story[6] the fact that it will be manufactured in our new acquisition, the Elmira plant? You would need a picture[7] of either the product or the process. Since the deadline is two weeks distant, you have a little[8] time in which to work; therefore, why not ask R and D for suggestions. (173)

138▶ Chamber of Commerce, Ashland, Kentucky 41101.

Gentlemen: We appreciate very much your assessment of the advantages of locating our new plant[1] in Ashland. The report was complete and yet concise. You are to be congratulated on your efforts to attract[2] new industry to your locality.

Our special committee established to recommend the site

best suited[3] to our needs, however, has asked me to tell you that we have eliminated Ashland from further[4] consideration.

Let me assure you again of our gratitude for your assistance in making this decision. Best[5] wishes to you in your continued efforts to develop Ashland into an industrial center. Yours truly,[6] (121)

139▶ To Arthur C. Williamson, Public Information Director, Subject: Purchase of Elmira Plant.

Mr. Simpson has authorized me to send you the following information:

This morning we received[1] final acceptance of our offer to purchase the Universal Can Company in Elmira, Ontario.[2] Knowing that you will want to prepare an immediate press release for distribution to your entire list[3] of 453 business periodicals and financial pages, I am providing the following[4] information on which the release can be based.

The purchase price is not to be revealed. The Universal[5] Can Company provides an excellent opportunity for needed diversification of our operations.[6] All types of containers, from tin cans to plastic and aerosol bottles, are manufactured at the[7] Elmira plant, which employs 450 workers. In addition to adding new products to a growing list[8] of items manufactured by National Products, this acquisition will enable our company to[9] manufacture its own containers for packaging its manufactured products. Production costs will thus be reduced[10] materially.

Favorable tariff concessions of the Canadian Government were a factor in[11] the decision of our company to negotiate this purchase.

Here is a photograph of the new plant in[12] Elmira. Twenty-five or so glossy prints might be made from this photograph for distribution with the press releases[13] to key members of the press. I shall be out of the office until two o'clock this afternoon. After[14] that you may telephone me or come to see me if you need additional details. (295)

Unit 7

Secretarial Assignment

1 After pining for recognition, he won unparalleled praise.
2 By reshaping the company's policy, the committee stepped up production.
3 The offering of preferred stock was canceled.
4 Recurring expenses compelled the company to raise prices.
5 He labeled the winning design as unequaled in the history of the company.
6 The new product rivaled any previously manufactured.
7 The directors concurred in approving the product modeled after ours.
8 The controller approved the new offering of preferred stock.
9 One way of combating auto-

mation is through increased production.

10 Profits this year totaled more than one million dollars.

11 Unparalleled benefits occurred from modeling our production methods after those of the parent company.

12 Controlled experiments are modeled after those that are already successful.

LESSON 31

1 Your sales statement for March, including the year-to-date totals, is enclosed.

2 The team's research findings, which were distributed widely, were debated by the Administrative Committee.

3 We must consider next year's budget estimate when you return.

4 The index cards, being in alphabetical order, are now ready for filing.

5 The company that diversifies its products has a better chance of survival.

6 Statistics, which is really not a difficult course, will benefit you.

7 Mr. Roberts, who works in the laboratory, will discuss his next assignment with you when he returns from his vacation.

8 I hope, John, that you can see me on Tuesday to discuss the proposal.

9 The contract that was signed and witnessed has been filed.

10 The order was shipped before your letter was received.

11 Miss Henry, who is an excellent secretary, is receiving a

promotion.

12 Any secretary who grows in understanding will probably receive recognition.

13 He agreed to submit specific recommendations when he returns from his inspection tour.

14 Statistics related to business forecasting will benefit you most.

15 You, Mr. Jones, are the best judge of that statement.

16 For the fifteenth time, will you please keep that window closed.

140▶ To: All Laboratory Foremen, Subject: Safety Precautions.

The July safety lesson will be a presentation on the importance of good housekeeping.

The members of[1] your Safety Committee have developed this lesson, and they will present it at the next regular foremen's meeting.[2] To ensure good attendance, we are asking each foreman to arrange his schedule in order to avoid[3] commitments on that date. We feel that this lesson is especially timely because of the importance of safety[4] precautions in research laboratories.

Considerable improvement has been made in the reduction of safety[5] hazards in the laboratory. Care in the storage of volatile materials, careful destruction of[6] residue from experiments, and adherence to the rules for wearing protective covering during tests can[7] be cited as examples of safety precautions.

Lost-time accidents and accidents involving medical[8] expense have decreased 5 percent over the first quarter of last year. A review of medical reports fails to[9] show any specific type of recurring accidents. It does, however, show a high incidence of such minor[10] accidents as burns, cuts, bruises, and sprains.

Many unnecessary accidents are caused by employees who[11] leave equipment in aisles, drawers or cabinets open, and flames unprotected. Let's be sure that all employees know[12] and practice safe work habits on all operations and that they take full advantage of our first-aid training and[13] equipment. The downward trend in accidents can be continued. You can help! (274)

141▶ Dr. Hubert C. Busch, Research and Development Department, National Products, Inc., 211 Forest Avenue, St. Louis, Missouri 63100.

Dear Doctor Busch: Congratulations on the success of your research team with Project 72, which has now[1] been approved for production by National Products. I am asking our patent attorneys to prepare the[2] application for a company patent on the manufacturing process finally adopted. They will[3] undoubtedly request your help in submitting completely accurate drawings and technical descriptions of the[4] process used.

We realize that you already hold the patent for the toggle switches used in the process. These[5] switches were developed

on your own time, and your patent fully protects your rights.

Our attorneys will discuss with[6] you the terms under which we can manufacture these toggle switches. As a preliminary to their meeting[7] with you, however, I suggest that you quote to me the royalty you would expect to receive for our use of[8] your patent in manufacturing Project 72.

You may expect to hear from the patent attorney[9] assigned to Project 72 within the next two weeks. This letter is to alert you to this next step in[10] getting Project 72 (and your invention) into production. Yours cordially, (216)

142▶ Dr. Harvey D. Bentley, The Bentley Research Center, 235 Greentree Road, Columbus, Ohio 43217.

Dear Doctor Bentley: We are sending you today by airfreight experimental materials on which you are[1] to run six tests of tensile strength according to the enclosed specifications. As you know, we do not have proper[2] equipment for running these tests.

We have been pleased with previous tests that you completed for us, and we know that[3] we can depend on you again for your usual high standard of performance.

As the project involved is at[4] a crucial stage of development, may we count on you to complete the tests and return the materials and[5] reports by airfreight by March 10? Please telephone me if there will be any delay beyond that date so that I[6] can reschedule the men assigned to this project. Yours very truly, (132)

143▶ Dr. Harvey D. Bentley, The Bentley Research Center, 235 Greentree Road, Columbus, Ohio 43217.

Dear Doctor Bentley: We appreciate very much your promptness in running our recent tests so quickly and so[1] expertly. We are willing to pay overtime to the technicians required for such emergency situations,[2] for we save money here in our laboratories by maintaining our original schedules in this way.[3]

The work of our Research and Development center is expedited because we know that we can depend on[4] your center to complete any tests we send you in record time and with strict adherence to our specifications.[5] Cordially yours, (102)

LESSON 32

144▶ Wellman Business Machine Company, 211 Bay State Road, Knoxville, Tennessee 37900.

Gentlemen: Do you produce an electrostatic copying machine capable of reproducing engineering[1] drawings 18 inches by 24 inches, with enlargement and reduction features? Our present machine[2] is an indirect photostatic process that requires about 60 seconds per copy and reproduces[3] on paper that does not have a sat-isfactory writing surface.

If one of your new dry-contact models will[4] satisfy our specialized copy requirements (assuming average operator skill and materials),[5] please deliver a demonstrator to our Research and Development Department for a 30-day trial.[6] Sincerely yours, (122)

145▶ To: All R and D Employees, Subject: Security.

Much of the competitive advantage National Products has acquired is due to its ability to keep[1] research projects secret. Perhaps it is inconceivable to some of you that competitors are constantly[2] scouting our laboratory for intelligence about our plans and progress in developing new products.[3]

Many of you have recently come to the laboratory from universities, where it is customary[4] to discuss your activities freely with colleagues. It is hard to realize that a careless remark could[5] cost your company hundreds of thousands of dollars if it were passed along to a rival manufacturer.[6]

Please guard your conversation about your work. Never discuss research projects outside the building. Say nothing about[7] experiments being conducted or product designs under consideration. In the laboratory[8] be sure to place blueprints and flow charts in locked files when they are not in use. Keep reminding yourself that new product[9] ideas are our most important investment in the future. Do not give them away. (195)

146▶ Williams, Henderson, and Brown, Attorneys at Law, Crescent Building, 440 Michigan Avenue, Chicago, Illinois 60610.

Gentlemen: Research and development operations have expanded rapidly at NATIONAL PRODUCTS. As[1] you might suspect, the company's investment is substantial. With this in mind, we believe that we should review the[2] contract that we ask our employees to sign with regard to the patent rights that NATIONAL PRODUCTS has to their[3] scientific efforts. In general, the present contract specifies that any invention made in the course[4] of employment in the Research and Development Department belongs to NATIONAL PRODUCTS.

Bear in mind that[5] we allow our employees more time than any of our competitors for what we call "puttering" but what might[6] more properly be called "sponsored creative effort." Any patents obtained for inventions made while an employee[7] is engaged in this sponsored research belong to us. Management feels that this interpretation cannot be[8] challenged. Admittedly, there is one obvious grey area in this logic: it is difficult — sometimes[9] impossible — to determine whether an idea was conceived on the job at 3:38 p.m. or during[10] dinner at 8:12 p.m.

Fortunately, we have not had any cases arise on the question of rights[11] to inventions. Occasionally we use an employee's patented invention on a job if he has developed[12] a superior component. I think, however, that it would be wise to review the present contract[13] in the light of possible legal involvement.

Please consult with the Patent Office before we plan a conference[14] to hear your recommendations. Sincerely yours, (290)

147▶ Dr. Irwin J. Miller, President, American Chemical Society, Massachusetts Technological Institute, 2444 Massachusetts Avenue, Boston, Massachusetts 02215.

Dear Doctor Miller: I shall be very happy to present a paper at the annual meeting of the[1] American Chemical Society in New Orleans on December 29, 30, and 31.[2] The title of the paper will be "X-ray Analysis of Molecules." A 500-word abstract will be[3] sent to you by December 1 for inclusion in Chemical Abstracts, as you requested. If you have a[4] suggested format for the abstract, please send it to me immediately; otherwise, I shall use last year's edition[5] as my guide.

Thank you very much for this opportunity to present my research to this most important[6] audience. Sincerely yours, (123)

* * *

▶ If you eliminate carbon copies for unimportant correspondence (acknowledgments, thank-yous, etc.,), you can avoid some unnecessary filing.

LESSON 33

148▶ To: Mr. Henry P. Walters,

Vice-President, Finance, Subject: Preliminary Budget Estimate.

You asked me for a suggested figure for the R and D budget for next year. My first step in trying to arrive[1] at a figure was to find out what other companies are budgeting for this purpose.

Manufacturers[2] in the field of electronics, aircraft, electrical and scientific instruments, and other space-age products[3] budget from 6 to 12 percent of annual sales for R and D. Food-processing and mining companies,[4] on the other hand, budget an average of only one-half of 1 percent of annual net sales for R[5] and D. Of the amount appropriated for development of new products and improvement of old ones, 5[6] percent is customarily spent on finding new breakthroughs and the other 95 percent on making new[7] applications of processes already known. This apportionment seems a wise guideline for us to follow.

As[8] our company manufactures a diversity of products, we should probably spend less for research than the[9] manufacturers of strictly new products but considerably more than the manufacturers of standard[10] ones. To maintain leadership in all the areas of production engaged in by National Products, I[11] recommend that we earmark 5 percent of our annual sales for R and D. Based on last year's net sales, this would give[12] us a budget of $1,250,000.

I believe, Mr. Walters, that with an[13] annual budget of $1,250,000, we could maintain a research and development[14] program that would keep National Products ahead of its competition in the development of new products[15] and in the refinement of existing ones.

I chose this method to justify the budget I have projected[16] rather than describe projects we should undertake, because management must first estimate the proportion of[17] annual sales that it is willing to reinvest in the form of research. After this has been done, priorities[18] can be assigned to projects. (365)

149▶ To: Mr. Arthur C. Williamson, Director of Public Information, Subject: Preliminary Demonstration of Project 77.

As you now know, Arthur, Project 77 is operational and we are ready to hold a[1] demonstration for the Administrative Committee in the laboratory at ten o'clock on Monday morning,[2] April 3.

Inasmuch as we are scientists and not display specialists, we must solicit your help in[3] preparing for this important presentation. Can you attend a Thursday morning preliminary demonstration?[4] At that time we can work out the details of the April 3 demonstration. Project 77 is, of[5] course, confidential. It will be some time before its identity will be released to the press and other[6] mass media.

Please let me know if you cannot work with me on Thursday morning. Do you mind if Dave Johnson, production[7] supervisor, is included in the dry run and discussion? He is thoroughly familiar with Project[8] 77 and has good ideas. My secretary will be on hand to take notes. (177)

150▶ Memo to Dr. Wilson Atwater, Senior Engineer, Subject: Project 328A.

Mr. Walters has asked me for our proposed budget request for next year. In my estimate I am suggesting[1] a figure based on 5 percent of sales, $1,250,000. I am recommending[2] that 5 percent of this amount be devoted to breakthroughs in the development of new products and that the[3] remaining 95 percent be used for finding new applications of present processes used in the[4] manufacture of National products. This distribution conforms to national averages, and I hope and expect[5] that Mr. Walters and the Administrative Committee will go along with my recommendation.

Under[6] this formula we would have $62,500 for the development of new products.

In[7] the original budgeting for Project 328A, we allotted your unit $100,000[8] to be used over a three-year period ending next March 31. Your progress reports indicate that[9] you will complete this work on schedule. I should like to know, however, whether any recent developments will[10] prevent your completing this project with the budgeted $8,500 for the three-month period.[11] I am collecting figures now so that I can move quickly in compiling the actual budget when I get[12] the go-ahead from Finance. (245)

LESSON 34

155▶ Mr. Robert Wilkinson, Chairman, School of Engineering, Washington University, Lindell and Skinker Boulevards, St. Louis, Missouri 63130.

Dear Bob: We have come to the point where our needs are so specialized that we plan to offer in-company technical[1] courses in addition to continuing our present policy of paying the tuition of our[2] engineers who complete job-related courses in your university.

To coordinate the two programs, we[3] plan to set up a council to advise us on such in-company courses.

Would you be willing to join this council?[4] Cordially yours, (83)

156▶ Mr. Milton G. McGill, Director, Research and Development, McMillan and King, Inc., 1110 Market Street, Duluth, Minnesota 55806.

Dear Milton: Do you remember the conversation we had at the Research and Development invitational[1] meeting at the University of Minnesota in February? Both of us were concerned with the[2] need for industry-supported laboratory facilities in some central university location[3] that we could use for running infrequent tests of a specialized nature. As we need the equipment only[4] occasionally, we could not economically justify purchasing it.

Do you still feel that the solution[5] to the problem is for eight or ten of the largest corporations in the area to endow such a laboratory[6] to be located in a university in the upper Middle Western region? If so, would you[7] be willing to serve on a committee to draft a proposal? Whom else do you suggest for the committee?

How[8] do you feel about restricting the use of the facilities to the contributors and the university[9] chosen, or should any company be allowed to make tests in the proposed laboratory? I shall be[10] interested in any further thoughts you may have had since our previous discussion. Sincerely yours, (218)

157▶ To: Alice E. Evans, Supervisor of In-Service Training, Subject: In-Service Courses for R and D Employees.

To provide in-service training that will ensure development of our R and D staff, I propose that they[1] be offered after-work courses during the year, beginning September 1.

Each class would meet for four hours a week[2] for eight weeks, possibly starting at 5:45 p.m. These courses should be taught either by our own senior[3] staff members, who would receive compensation, or by faculty members from the universities in the area.[4] As these programs are highly specialized, would you be willing for me to staff them once we have agreed on[5] the course offerings

and the budget? In my opinion, we could have a minimum enrollment of 20 employees[6] in each of the courses offered.

Four courses would serve our immediate needs:

Advanced Programming
Experimental[7] Design
Advanced Linear Algebra
Nuclear Physics

In addition, National Products would[8] continue to pay the tuition costs of any R and D employee who completes satisfactorily[9] an approved job-related course at Washington University, St. Louis University, or Loyola[10] University.

If you agree that mathematics and physics courses should be given on the premises,[11] do you want to make the recommendation to Mr. Simpson in your capacity as supervisor[12] of in-service training, or do you feel that such courses properly belong in the domain of research and[13] development? If you take the latter view, I shall be glad to present the request to Mr. Simpson. I want you[14] to understand, though, that I do not want in any way to usurp your prerogative.

Will you please give some thought[15] to this recommendation and to the best way of implementing it. Would you join me for lunch on June 10 to[16] discuss the details of this proposal? (327)

160▶ Memo to Mary Hendrix, Research Librarian, Subject: Bordered Paper Towels.

On April 3 I must submit to our company president a blueprint for needed research for our acquisition,[1] the Universal Can Company.

The recent development of decorative borders on paper[2] towels may provide an interesting and profitable opportunity for diversification of[3] products in our new factory. Will you please locate all possible information on this development for[4] consideration by our planning group. I am especially interested in the contribution of graphic[5] sciences to the perfection of a satisfactory process for the application of such borders[6] to paper towels and in any reports of consumer reaction to this innovation.

Because of the[7] urgency of our decision, your report must be received by February 9. (135)

LESSON 35

161▶ To: Mr. Henry M. Simpson, President, Subject: Research Recommendations.

On January 6 you requested that I make recommendations for research to be undertaken as[1] a result of our acquisition of the Universal Can Company, I spent two weeks in the Elmira[2] plant, and I have researched all available printed material about new trends in packaging. I also[3] spent two days in New York at a trade show on packaging. The librarian in our patent library is preparing[4] a report for my consideration.

The following two impressions have emerged from this preliminary[5] study, but I have only scratched the surface, of course.

1. The potential for developing new containers[6] of many types is tremendous. Old-fashioned tin plate has been supplanted by thin tin or aluminum as[7] the raw material from which cans are made. Containers of paper, plastic, and fiber foil are being used increasingly[8] in place of cans. Aerosol cans now dispense everything from cake icing to liquid bandages.[9] Plastic bags in which frozen foods can be cooked are a recent innovation. In many companies the container[10] rather than the product in it receives the advertising emphasis.

2. Competition in the container[11] field is very keen. One of the major manufacturers has allocated 10 percent of sales to R[12] and D for next year. Some of the largest packers are beginning to manufacture their own cans and thus remove[13] themselves as customers. Several container manufacturers are exploring foreign markets as a way[14] to increase sales. Success in this area depends on many unpredictable factors.

Here is my first[15] recommendation:

Because of both facilities and staff, research on containers to be manufactured in the[16] Universal Can Company factory should be moved immediately to our research and development[17] laboratory here in St. Louis. If you agree, this move can be accomplished by July 1.

A blueprint covering[18] additional research needs will require more time, but you may expect to receive one by April 1.[19] (380)

Unit 8————————————

Secretarial Assignment

1 For centuries collectors experienced difficulties in identifying old masters.
2 The attorneys expressed annoyance at the betrayal of the trust.
3 By modifying the pattern, we were able to save pennies on the project.
4 Inventories are heavily reduced by the Christmas holidays.
5 He hurriedly carried off the copies of the inventory.
6 The person who pinches pennies does not necessarily amass the biggest fortune.
7 She copied the testimonial for the proper authorities.
8 Of all the journeys I ever made, I found the one through the Valleys of the Kings the most satisfying.
9 After the holidays the secretaries found their work heavier.
10 The armies of our allies carried their share of the burden.
11 I am relying on you to prevent annoyances about losing the keys.
12 The authorities were dissatisfied with the hurried examination of luggage.
13 Heavy losses accompanied the victories of the armies.

1 He lived in Ohio but worked in Tennessee.
2 He lived in Cincinnati, Ohio, but worked in Covington, Kentucky.
3 My aunt Mary is visiting in St. Louis, Missouri, for two weeks.
4 After July we shall adopt a new vacation policy.
5 After August 1, 1965, the new tariff policy goes into effect.
6 A complicated, expensive plan for production in the San Francisco plant was approved.
7 My secretary, Mrs. Bell, who has been with me since July 15, 1959, is leaving.
8 We considered a site in Columbus, Ohio, but decided against it.
9 Mr. Brown, our auditor, can be reached in Boston if necessary.
10 After the shipment left Chicago on July 7, the engine was derailed.
11 We located your letter of May 2, 1963, and verified the figures.
12 Mr. Wilson, who has been with our company since 1962, was promoted today.
13 We are transferring your friend Williams from our San Diego, California, plant.
14 My sister Joan works for a sophisticated downtown public-relations firm.
15 The product is manufactured in Knoxville, Tennessee, but marketed through the Skokie, Illinois, headquarters.
16 He became eligible for retirement on June 2 and left the company.

162▶ Lake Erie Steel Company, 200 Richmont Avenue, Toledo, Ohio 43637.

Gentlemen: On June 7 we mailed you our Purchase Order No. 834 for three carloads of sheet metal to[1] be delivered by August 8 to our St. Louis headquarters. Yesterday a fire destroyed the warehouse that had[2] been allocated for this shipment. It is necessary, therefore, to delay delivery of this order[3] until November 8, at which time our storage facilities will be completely rebuilt.

During this three-month[4] period our stock of sheet metal will be trucked in from various branch warehouses and our production levels[5] will be maintained. Except during a one-week slowdown in production, while we are setting up new stock-delivery[6] schedules, we expect to meet all production commitments.

So that your company will not be inconvenienced[7] by our misfortune, please bill us for the three carloads of sheet metal as originally purchased. Your company[8] should not suffer because delivery on this order must be delayed for a three-month period. We do[9] hope, though, that you will allow the trade discount that we would have earned if the order had been executed as[10] originally planned. Sincerely yours, (207)

163▶ Mr. Harman J. Cooper, Cooper Office Furniture Company, 2511 Belltown Road, Jamestown, New York 14701.

Dear Mr. Cooper: Can you deliver 150 stenographic desks, Model 197, in time for[1] the opening of our Albany branch office on August 20?

Thirty-five of these desks are to be beige[2] with no-glare Formica tops; the remaining 115, in standard office grey with metal tops. All of[3] them, however, are to be equipped with the custom-made file drawer shown on the enclosed drawing. We have used Model[4] 197 in several of our installations and have found it to be very satisfactory for[5] both general office use and mid-management use.

A purchase order will not be issued until you have had[6] an opportunity to check your production schedules. We fully realize that a three-week notice may not[7] be adequate for an order of this magnitude. We were unable, however, to anticipate our exact[8] need until the office layouts for the new branch were complete. Sincerely yours, (174)

164▶ Almark Metal Products, Inc., 722 Division Street, Mansfield, Ohio 44902.

Gentlemen: We are interested in contracting for a year's supply of die-cut gears manufactured from alloy[1] steel cut to the specifications given on the enclosed blueprint. We expect to use 120,000[2] of these gears every month in manufacturing an assortment of vending machines.

Our decision to purchase[3] the gears from you depends on your answers to the following questions:

1. What is your best price per one thousand gears?[4]

2. Can you guarantee monthly delivery if we place an order with you?

3. What trade discount can you allow?[5]

4. In case we increase our production, is there a quantity beyond which you would be unable to[6] guarantee delivery?

5. What quality control would you exercise over the manufacture of these gears?[7]

We hope that your replies will make it possible for us to purchase gears from your company. Yours very truly,[8] (160)

165▶ Williamson Chemical Company, Berea Road, Lexington, Kentucky 40505.

Gentlemen: Please send us color charts of dyes for use with Dacron materials. From these charts we shall select colors[1] that we wish to sample before placing an order. We are especially concerned about getting a true[2] dye for various shades of blue.

Please quote quantity prices of your dyes and any quantity discounts allowed.[3] Any suggestions for improving our dyeing of Dacron will be appreciated. Yours very truly,[4] (80)

* * *

▶ Have two notebooks on your desk — one for dictation and the other left open to a clean page for short notes and last-minute instructions. You can quickly jot down notes without looking for a clean page in the notebook from which you are transcribing.

166▶ To: Mr. Henry P. Walters, Senior Vice-President, Subject: European Trade Fairs.

I have been studying the industrial, trade, and technical publications of Western Europe in a search[1] for possible suppliers of metal fabricating materials at prices low enough to interest[2] us.

Unlike manufacturers in the United States, European manufacturers count on trade fairs as[3] their principal key to markets. Small European capital goods manufacturers may concentrate almost[4] their entire sales efforts on a given fair, planning on selling at one time almost their total production[5] capacity for the period between fairs.

What would you think of my attending several such fairs in April?[6] I could include four consecutive events in one itinerary without being out of the country for[7] longer than one month.

Probably the most famous of these fairs is the annual spring industrial exposition[8] in Hanover, Germany. The dates this year are April 4 to 10. This event could be followed by the fair[9] in Copenhagen, Denmark, from April 12 to 17. The London trade exposition will be held from April[10] 16 to 24. I would have to backtrack to the Continent for the final fair in Milan, Italy,[11] from April 25 to 30.

The publications indicate that prices are favorable. I am not[12] sure, however, that we can bring purchases into the United States without so much tariff involvement that[13] the effort would be justified. Do you know a foreign-trade adviser at one of the banks with which we do business[14] to whom we could go for advice? Would you prefer to talk with someone alone, or would you suggest that both of[15] us confer with him to discuss the feasibility of my suggestion?

Your thoughts on this matter will be[16] appreciated. (321)

167▶ BBB Manufacturing Company, 216 Broad Street, Indianapolis, Indiana 46241.

Gentlemen: On July 6 we ordered 150 heavy-duty suction pumps from your company at[1] the price you quoted in a letter dated July 1. You can imagine our reaction when we read in the[2] newspapers on July 7 that your company would reduce the price of these suction pumps 20 percent effective[3] July 14.

For the past twelve years our business with you has been based on our belief in the integrity[4] of your management as well as on our belief that quality is your major product consideration. Because[5] of these convictions we wonder why you did not give a good customer the benefit of a substantial[6] reduction in price on an order given only one day before the public announcement.

We believe that you[7] should allow us to purchase these pumps at the reduced price. In view of our past business relations, we urge you to[8] recon-

sider the issue involved and then send us a revised billing. Sincerely yours, (176)

168▶ To: All Section Heads, Subject: Form of Purchase Requisition.

In completing requisitions for office supplies, please indicate the quality of supply you need, not the[1] brand name. For instance, specify that you want 20-pound bond paper rather than Hawk Bond, that you want No. 2[2] lead pencils rather than McMann pencils.

Do not complete the column headed "Source." The reason for this request is[3] that we buy in terms of both quality and price. Because of quantity buying, we may be able to obtain[4] a quality superior to that requested but at a lower price than we could obtain from the company[5] designated.

The exception to this policy is in ordering typewriter ribbons. Because of the[6] diversity of models in use throughout our offices, we request that you specify both the make of[7] typewriter and the model. If you have any difficulty in getting the right ribbons for certain machines, you[8] may have to give the serial number of the machine; but such cases are rare.

Do not write in the column headed[9] "Amount." The figures for that column will be inserted in this office. (194)

169▶ Watterson Electronics, 29 Waters View Drive, Bridgeport, Connecticut 06614, Attention of James R. Mitchell.

Gentlemen: The enclosed Purchase Order No. 7143 confirms our order placed by telephone today.[1] The emergency was created by a warehouse fire in which our entire supply of electronic components[2] used in the manufacture of dictating equipment was destroyed.

We appreciate your assurance that[3] you will rush the first third of the order to us by airfreight on July 16, the earliest date by which you[4] can complete the manufacture of the goods. Thank you. Yours very truly, (93)

LESSON 38

170▶ Griswold Manufacturing Company, 448 Spring Hill Road, Wheeling, West Virginia 26001.

Gentlemen: On March 7 we received your shipment of 100 dozen packing boxes. The packing slip refers[1] to a Purchase Order No. 43227, dated March 5.

Apparently an error has been made by[2] your shipping department. We have screened our purchase orders and were unable to locate this order. In fact, we[3] have not ordered boxes of any type since we received our year's supply from you on January 6.

Please let[4] us know what disposition you wish made of this shipment. Sincerely yours, (93)

171▶ M & L Steel Company, 245 Second Avenue, Pittsburgh, Pennsylvania 15212.

Gentlemen: Thank you for your partial shipment on our Order No. 6001. It will take care of our needs[1] temporarily; but, if at all possible, we hope you can arrange to ship one-half of our order next week[2] from your Birmingham branch. As you know, we allotted this sizable order to your company with the understanding[3] that one-fourth of the steel would be delivered each month from November through February. It is now[4] December 2, and we have received only one-eighth of our order.

Our production schedule includes the manufacture[5] of steel cables during the months of January and February. Unless we receive steel from you according[6] to the terms of our purchase order, however, we shall have to revise this schedule or take immediate[7] steps to get the steel elsewhere. In either case, valuable production time will be lost.

We prefer to deal[8] with you because in the past we have been able to rely on your shipment schedules. However, our situation[9] is growing desperate. Please let us know promptly whether you will be able to meet your commitment next week and[10] during the following months. Yours very truly, (209)

172▶ The Bradshaw Chemical Company, 900 Plains Boulevard, Houston, Texas 77021.

Gentlemen: Our quality control engineer, Mr. Raymond C. Rankin, reports that his routine tests show that[1] the current mixture of our commercial fertilizer ALFGROW is not meeting min-

66

imum production standards.[2] The percentage of spoilage greatly exceeds the statistical limits under which this popular brand fertilizer[3] is produced.

Mr. Rankin's chemical analysis indicates that the ammonium hydroxide[4] supplied by your company for use in ALFGROW does not conform to the specifications written into our[5] purchase order of October 17. We have used your ammonium hydroxide in manufacturing[6] 10,000 tons of fertilizer that we must now condemn.

Please cancel the undelivered portion of our Purchase[7] Order No. 1173. In addition, we suggest that you send your sales engineer to discuss the[8] necessary adjustment on the portion of the order responsible for the product loss we have suffered.[9] Yours very truly, (183)

173▶ Hammer Paint & Building Supplies, Inc., 5734 North Pacific Avenue, San Diego, California 92111.

Gentlemen: Enclosed are two photographs of the paint sprayer that we have used for many years in applying your[1] paint X64 in our machine finishing room. One shows the sprayer in closed position, and the other shows it[2] almost open. In the closed position the sprayer is about 10 inches long; extended, it is about twice[3] that length.

We wish to replace the sprayers; but here in St. Louis, the supply houses have not been able to supply[4] a duplicate of this model, which has given such excellent results on the fin-ishing of our metal[5] drums. We are told this sprayer is no longer manufactured.

Can you furnish us with this type of sprayer? If[6] not, can you recommend a substitute make and model that would be appropriate for your X64 paint?

Any[7] guidance that you can give us in resolving this replacement problem will be appreciated, for we want[8] to continue to get the same excellent results with your paint. Sincerely yours, (174)

174▶ Harmon and Bowman Steel Corporation, 231 Beacon Drive, Cleveland, Ohio 44122.

Gentlemen: Please quote prices of steel conforming to the enclosed specifications in the quantity lots[1] indicated.

One of the primary considerations in our decision about buying from your company[2] is your guarantee that you can begin delivery of at least 100 tons a week by December 20[3] and continue throughout January and February.

Since time is of the essence, please telephone your[4] quotation as soon as you have assembled the necessary information. Yours truly, (97)

LESSON 39

179▶ Hadley Machine Tooling Company, 275 Euclid Avenue, Erie, Pennsylvania 16518.

Gentlemen: For the past five years we have been purchasing many of the fabricating machines used in NATIONAL[1]

PRODUCTS plants from your company. All these purchases have been on open account.

Our maintenance personnel[2] service these machines, and we purchase all replacement parts from you. Your policy has been to ship parts on sight draft[3] or C.O.D. This is very inconvenient, as it sometimes delays the receipt of parts that are needed[4] for emergency repairs. In addition to extra paper work, your policy occasionally involves[5] an otherwise unnecessary trip to our bank.

We prefer to obtain replacement parts on open account.[6] If you wish to have additional credit data, please send your application form to our credit manager,[7] Mr. Harold C. Poling. Sincerely yours, (148)

180▶ Larkin Engineers, 422 Second Street, Eau Claire, Wisconsin 54701.

Gentlemen: Recently NATIONAL PRODUCTS acquired the Diamond Can Company, in Elmira, Ontario.[1] During the next six months we are planning to convert a portion of this plant into a plastic bottle division.[2] Your company has been suggested as one that could custom-build the assembly line of molds for shaping plastic[3] bottles.

Specifications for the installation have been completed. If you are interested in undertaking[4] the job, we would want you to send a sales engineer to examine the plans and specifications. If a[5] preliminary discussion is mutually satisfactory,

an inspection tour of the Elmira[6] plant would be scheduled. At that time your engineers could study the installation problem and confer with me[7] and a number of our production personnel.

Please wire me as soon as you can whether Larkin Engineers is[8] in a position at this time to undertake this project. Sincerely yours, (174)

181▶ Memo to Stuart P. Henderson, Advertising Manager, Subject: Requisition No. 78779.

Your Requisition No. 78779 for snap-out forms for production schedules specifies the Kennedy[1] Paper Company as the source of these forms, which must be custom-printed to meet our needs.

May I suggest that[2] we place this order with Northern Paper Products, which now prints the snap-out forms used in Administrative Services[3] and in Accounting. There are three reasons for wanting to use this vendor:

1. It quotes consistently lower[4] prices than its competitors, especially the Kennedy Paper Company.

2. Its quantity discounts[5] are also advantageous.

3. We can get better service if we buy all printed forms from one company.

I[6] would not change your requisition, though, without inquiring whether there is some technical advantage of the[7] Kennedy forms that I do not recognize. If there is, please let me know what it is. (154)

182▶ Memo to John Parker, Administrative Services, Subject: Requisition No. 273.

I know that nobody in the company appreciates the advantages of standardizing our equipment[1] more than you do, John. Reducing the number of different makes of typewriters in the different offices[2] is important for a number of reasons; yet your Requisition No. 273 requests the purchase[3] of a German typewriter that has recently received high ratings by the Buyers' Laboratory, which conducts[4] endurance tests for its members.

I have telephoned the manufacturer's representative and find that no[5] service contract is available on this machine.

Although I realize that the machine you requisitioned[6] has a high reputation for durability, may I suggest that under the circumstances you change your[7] specification to one of the two typewriters used throughout the rest of the offices. In this way we can not[8] only assure adequate service on our machines, but we can also reduce service costs. (177)

183▶ The McBride Corporation, 4100 Gulf Street, Baytown, Texas 77520.

Gentlemen: NATIONAL PRODUCTS is preparing to manufacture an electric broiler, and we should like to[1] inquire about components that you can furnish. Complete specifications, together with the quantities we[2] expect to need during the next six months, are enclosed.

If you are interested, please send us samples of any[3] parts that you can supply. Also, quote prices in quantity lots of 5,000, 10,000, and 20,000[4] as well as proposed delivery dates.

Inasmuch as production of the electric broiler is scheduled to[5] begin in four weeks, we shall appreciate your prompt reply. Sincerely yours, P.S. Please send six copies of your[6] current catalog to our production manager, Mr. James W. Walsh. (133)

LESSON 40

186▶ To: William C. Wilson, Foreman, Shipping Department, Subject: Requisition 743.

Requisition 743, dated July 18, requests 1,000 dozen wooden boxes, 12 by 36[1] inches.

You have never before ordered more than 100 dozen boxes of this type at one time. We wonder[2] whether you have storage space for such a large shipment.

Is it possible that your stenographer made a mistake[3] and that you intended to order 100 dozen boxes as usual? Did you intend to requisition[4] the 1,000 dozen and specify staggered delivery?

To take care of your immediate needs, in the[5] event your present supply is low, I am ordering 100 dozen. The remainder of your order will[6] be withheld, pending your clarification of need. (129)

187▶ To: Charles C. Haynes, Di-

rector, **Research and Development, Subject: Project 72.**

Now that Project 72 has been approved for production, I am preparing to order the materials[1] to be used.

Your report outlining the formulae and specifications has been studied, but a number[2] of specifics remain unanswered. To expedite the processing of this order, would you please review your[3] specifications and then supply any additional details as to quality of materials that should[4] be included in our purchase orders.

It would also be helpful in deciding on quantities to be ordered[5] if you could give me information about rate of deterioration of the various components.[6]

We do have some data that relates to the purchases made while the project was being developed in your[7] laboratory; however, changes have been made, and I must rely on you to spell them out if we are to get the[8] best materials for this project. (165)

**188▶ Office Furnishings Inc.,
410 Olive Street, St. Louis, Missouri 63102.**

Gentlemen: On May 11, 1966, you sold us ten secretarial chairs, Model 15A,[1] manufactured by the Lifton Company, of Minneapolis. These chairs are adjustable in height.

Apparently,[2] the threads on the pedestal by which the seats are raised and lowered are defective. On four of the chairs the seats[3] can no longer be moved in either direction by turning the metal part at the base of the chair by hand.

Since[4] we have used the chairs only one year, we think that you will want to make an adjustment. Shall I expect one of your[5] trucks to pick up the chairs for your inspection, or will your representative examine them in our home office?[6] We should prefer the latter solution, as we shall need the chairs during the period of adjustment. Yours very[7] truly, (141)

189▶ Lifton Company, 816 Second Avenue, Minneapolis, Minnesota 55405.

Gentlemen: On May 11 of last year, we bought ten secretarial chairs, Model 15A, from Office[1] Furnishings Inc., of St. Louis. Although the chairs have been used only one year, four of them can no[2] longer be adjusted because the threads on the pedestal by which the seats can be moved up or down have worn so[3] badly that they do not hold.

We expected that Office Furnishings Inc. would make an adjustment.[4] In fact, we hoped that they would replace all ten chairs with satisfactory ones — with a cash payment from us for[5] wear. However, we received the following reply to our request: "Since these chairs were not guaranteed and since you[6] used them a full year, we can make no adjustment."

We are now writing you because we feel that your dealer in this[7] area is not representing your company as you would wish it represented. We have been buying Lifton[8] furniture for years for our branches and factories throughout the United States. We should like to continue[9] to buy from you, but we cannot do so if we cannot get an adjustment on defective items.

Can you suggest[10] a solution? Yours very truly, (205)

190▶ Truxton Products, 299 Dearborn Avenue, Detroit, Michigan 48252.

Gentlemen: Our Receiving Department reports that the electrical units that you have been shipping to us are[1] often received in a damaged condition. Apparently, the corrugated containers used are not properly[2] reinforced, because the top and sides are frequently punctured.

Perhaps you should use a container of a[3] heavier weight or an inner liner that would protect the electrical units in the event that the outer[4] covering was pierced.

By calling this problem to your attention, we hope you can take the necessary action[5] that will substantially reduce the number of damaged units we have been returning to you for credit. Sincerely[6] yours, (121)

Unit 9

Secretarial Assignment

1 This upholstery material has been judged serviceable.

2 The extraordinary results are directly traceable to his leadership.

3 He is too excitable to be put in charge of the unit.

4 After the fire alarm had been given, the workers became panicky.

5 He was always politicking for a 35-hour week and additional paid holidays.

6 Rather than agree to the outrageous demands, he resigned.

7 Management discovered that it had signed an unenforcible contract.

8 The purchasing agent pointed out that the interchangeable type faces were replaceable.

9 The foreman's position became untenable when the unmanageable workers mimicked him.

10 It would be advantageous for all hikers to wear serviceable shoes.

11 He was asked whether his conclusion was provable or whether it was still debatable.

12 The annual company outing gives every employee an opportunity to enjoy picnicking.

LESSON 41

1 Our quality standards, for instance, surpass those of comparable companies.

2 Frequently these matters become obscured.

3 We thought that the explanation was clear but realize that some people might choose to misunderstand it.

4 As a result, we must revise

the route sheet for the entire run.

5 He said that he had received the bill but admitted that he had mislaid it.

6 To begin with, it should be understood that we have been experimenting with the model.

7 Suddenly we found ourselves in serious trouble.

8 I attended the conference this year, but I shall not attend next year.

9 You might try reading Business Week, for instance.

10 I hope that this explanation is clear and anticipate that you will accept it.

11 In the first place, I don't accept your basic premise.

12 As a matter of fact, the newspapers reported the proceedings.

13 We believe that business will improve, and we hope that the year will end with the biggest profit in our history.

14 The president stated that profits had increased 12 percent and that further expansion is planned.

15 Surprisingly, I am not nervous about the interview.

16 On the other hand, your reasoning is perfectly clear.

191▶ To: Ralph C. Akin, Sales Manager, Subject: Factory Closing for Vacation.

Our summer vacation period is only three months away, and we need to make final plans for taking care[1] of seasonal and continuous-run product demands during this time.

For a number of years we tried staggering[2] vacations through the spring and summer months, but this plan slowed production and made it difficult to give customers[3] the products they wanted when they wanted them. Because we manufacture so many seasonal products, we[4] experimented last year by closing the entire plant for two weeks for vacations. This year the Administrative[5] Committee has approved the recommendation that our St. Louis operation be closed for vacations[6] during the period starting July 16 and extending through July 27.

With this in mind, Ralph, we[7] are revising our production schedules in order to meet our order commitments. Our objectives are twofold:[8] First, we expect to have our job-lot Christmas lines processed by July 1. Second, we shall step up production of[9] our continuous orders by 10 percent, stockpiling these items to cover normal demands during the two-week[10] period.

May I ask, Ralph, that you check your present orders for continuous-run products to see whether[11] they seem to conform to the usual pattern of demand for the two weeks when we shall be closed. If you will[12] cooperate by estimating your needs, we believe that we shall be able to meet all delivery promises.[13] To provide a small emergency inventory, we shall, of course, produce overruns; but our margin of[14] available products will be below normal during the vacation period.

We have a small amount of[15] unscheduled machine capacity

that could be utilized for job-lot orders before July 15. We [16] would need to have any special orders for customers buying items prepared to their own specifications [17] almost immediately, however, in order to handle them.

Please tell your salesmen of these plans promptly [18] so that our "delivery on time" objective can be achieved. (372)

192▶ Mr. Byron J. Brown, New York Hilton Hotel, Avenue of the Americas at 53rd Street, New York, New York 10019.

Dear Mr. Brown: Your sales manager, Mr. Ralph Akin, has asked me to give you a possible delivery [1] date for the Webber order, on which you are working as sales engineer.

After checking with our scheduling and [2] machine-capacity clerks, I can now tell you that we can guarantee delivery by February 1 [3] if the order, with complete specifications, is placed before November 9. We must know almost immediately, [4] however, whether or not we have the contract if we are to meet this deadline.

Another sales engineer [5] is bidding for a job lot that would tie up the equipment during the period that would be covered by [6] the Webber contract. It will be impossible to handle both contracts; so we can take only the one that is [7] completed first.

In your negotiations with the Webber people, be sure to stress the necessity for getting [8] the specifications to us prompt-

ly. The schedule that I have given you is a pretty tight one, and we may [9] have some difficulty in procuring the necessary raw materials. Sincerely yours, (197)

193▶ Mr. Elmer Weeks, Lennox Motor Inn, 1811 London Road, Duluth, Minnesota 55812.

Dear Mr. Weeks: I know that you are working on a job-lot contract with Hinton Distributors that would involve [1] one-third of our machine capacity from January 3 to 25. It looks now as if another [2] sales engineer may secure another order that would tie up all our equipment during that period.

Would [3] Hinton Distributors be willing to delay delivery until March 1? I do not want to interfere [4] with the Sales Department; and if suggesting this new date would jeopardize your chances of completing the sale, ignore [5] my request. The company signing the contract first gets the equipment. But if it does not really make a [6] difference to Hinton Distributors if delivery is postponed, will you please try to make the change. Both contracts [7] are lucrative, and we should mesh the production schedules if we can do so. Yours very cordially, (158)

LESSON 42

194▶ To: Henry E. Wilson, Plant Engineer, Subject: Conveyor Replacement.

Yes, I agree that we must replace the conveyor in Storeroom 6 immediately. Fortunately, there is[1] no problem, for it is included in our new budget for $5,600.

Before I requisition it,[2] however, I should want your recommendation as to the one you want. Will you please investigate the conveyors[3] available within our price range and report your findings to me. We can then make the final decision[4] together. (81)

195▶ To: Walter L. Hayes, Factory Superintendent, Subject: Factory Output.

I have just reviewed your monthly summary, Walter, and want to congratulate you on the increased output in[1] Departments 6, 8, and 11. Undoubtedly, the 10-hour induction training for new employees is paying[2] off in greater productivity by newly assigned workers.

If we can get better performance in Department[3] 9 next month, we can really feel that our major problems are solved. You are probably right in thinking[4] that it will be necessary to replace the foreman in that department before we can make substantial gains,[5] but I should like to give him one more month in which to prove himself. Another possible solution to the[6] problem of low individual output in that department might be the development of an in-service training[7] program for regular workers in the department. Let's discuss the next step when we see next month's summary.[8] (160)

196▶ To: Henry P. Walters, Senior Vice-President, Subject: Unit Cost, Product 17.

Today I received your authorization for a 50 percent increase in production of Product 17[1] and a copy of your approval for the purchase of raw materials.

One item, however, has been[2] overlooked in the estimates submitted. Our personnel and machines are already scheduled to capacity,[3] and it will be necessary to put on a second shift and possibly a third to meet the production[4] schedule that has been set up. Our rate for these night shifts is 50 cents an hour higher than the day rate, so that unit[5] costs will be 3 cents apiece higher than they are now.

Our budget, then, must be increased[6] $1,587.50 for the next two months. Because this is a considerable sum, I shall await your[7] approval before going ahead with the route cards and hiring the additional workers. (157)

197▶ McCormick Machinery Corporation, 411 West Lake Drive, Milwaukee, Wisconsin 53217 (Teletype Message).

Breakdown of Model 411 in Auxiliary Building 5, Concourse Plaza, St. Louis. Rush two hydraulic[1] shafts by automobile to arrive before 11 a.m. today with your installation engineer. If[2] you don't have repair parts, get them elsewhere. Emergency. Appreciate cooperation. (57)

198▶ To: Frederick C. Willis, Supervisor, Paint Shop, Sub-

ject: Repainting Rejects.

We are experiencing unusually high wastage on Products 117 and 335. I have asked[1] our inspection crew to study the rejects during the past month. They report that 75 percent of Product[2] 117 and 40 percent of Product 335 can be made salable by repainting.

The backlog[3] of rejects is being sent to you for a spray job, along with the route cards. After the backlog has been repainted,[4] future rejects will come to you as an added step on the route card. The satisfactory goods will be released,[5] and the rejects will be sent to you. (108)

199▶ To: William S. King, Plant Service Manager, Subject: Ordering Point.

Because of the instability of business conditions since January, the Administrative Committee[1] has authorized a change in the ordering point of all raw materials in this plant. The chances of[2] inflation make it advisable to stockpile materials in all departments.

Will you please issue a directive[3] to all stores-record clerks telling them to raise the point for reordering materials by 15 percent[4] until further notice. (83)

LESSON 43

200▶ To: All Department Foremen, Subject: Schedule for Job Order 89723, Jones & Miller.

The attached route card outlines the production schedule for Job No. 89723. When your department has[1] completed its assignment, please initial the master route card in the Check column, being sure to include the[2] date of completion. Send it immediately to the department foreman in charge of the next operation.[3]

If for any reason you are unable to meet the deadline for your operation, get in touch with me[4] immediately. (81)

201▶ To: Department Heads, Subject: Headache Workshop.

Come one — come all — to the quarterly luncheon on Thursday, February 3, in Executive Dining Room[1] No. 2. The luncheon is complimentary, but return the enclosed card by January 28 to[2] let us know you'll be present.

Be prepared to discuss, lament, and belabor your favorite supervisory[3] headache. You may even find a solution to eliminate the problem *and* the headache.

Selected foremen[4] have been asked to lead and stimulate the discussion at individual tables; they will use recorders to[5] report your recommendations to the group as a whole at the conclusion of the discussion.

Please indicate[6] your favorite headache in 1-2-3 order on the reply card so that the committee can seat you with a[7] group sharing your problems.

In order for the program to be successful, it will be essential for all foremen[8] to try to attend and participate so that ideas, techniques, and suggestions can be pooled.

Favorite Headaches:[9] (1) Absenteeism; (2) Obsolescence of Skills; (3) Pilfering; (4) Personnel (Quality and Availability);[10] (5) Salary Administration; (6) Tardiness; (7) Downtime; and (8) Failure to maintain schedule[11] as outlined on route cards. (225)

202▶ Mr. Charles C. Metchell, Production Manager, Atlas Manufacturing Company, Galveston, Texas 77552.

Dear Chuck: In the past we have often compared notes on common problems encountered on our jobs. You won't be surprised,[1] I hope, at this request for a summary of your experience in controlling raw materials and processed[2] products in your storerooms.

Here at our St. Louis plant we have been having unusually high wastage. I[3] believe, although conclusive evidence is not available, that most of it is caused by pilfering and by[4] attempts on the part of both foremen and workmen to make use of unaccountable waste material. On the[5] other hand, I am not ruling out thievery, which may be going on undetected.

We are, of course, tightening[6] our security measures. It occurred to me, however, that you may have encountered this problem in your[7] plant. In coping with it you may have devised controls that were effective. I seem to remember a discussion[8] of this problem at our meeting in Chicago last year. If this is the case, would you be good enough to tell me[9] how your company controls this problem.

Warm personal regards to you and your fine family. I do hope that[10] we can spend some time together while attending the Production Manager's Association Workshop in Pittsburgh[11] on November 26 and 27. Sincerely yours, (232)

203▶ Memo to Arthur Fleece, Training Department, Subject: Department Heads' Headache Workshop.

I am enclosing the announcement of the Headache Workshop that you were so helpful in planning. Fortunately,[1] it has been received with enthusiasm by department heads. Most of the foremen whom we asked have accepted[2] our invitation to lead the discussion at the eight tables. Eleven department heads have expressed their preference[3] for the discussion on obsolescence of skills. However, Ted Lanham feels that he cannot chair this discussion[4] and has asked that you serve in his place.

I know that you wanted to observe rather than participate so that you[5] could pinpoint the training needs as revealed in the discussion. However, most department heads perform better than[6] they talk and are reluctant to speak publicly; therefore, I should appreciate your acting as leader instead[7] of Ted.

You establish rapport with the men quickly; and once you

get under way, Arthur, I feel sure that you can act[8] as chairman and still secure the information you need. (170)

LESSON 44

208▶ KMC Communications Corporation, 211 Randolph Avenue, St. Paul, Minnesota 55131.

Gentlemen: Please send your sales engineer to discuss the possible use of computerized operations in[1] the manufacture of ALFGROW, our commercial fertilizer.

Last week I saw your installation at the[2] chemical division of the Marathon Oil Company, and I believe that adoption of automated equipment[3] would similarly reduce our production costs.

When he is here, I should like your representative to[4] meet with members of our Administrative Committee individually to describe the processes used[5] in computerized mixing and the quality control standards you can achieve with this equipment. To sell our[6] management on this installation will be difficult, and a formal presentation is premature. I believe,[7] though, that informal individual conferences over a two-day period would be effective.[8]

Please let me know when you can schedule this visit. Sincerely yours, (172)

209▶ Memo to Mr. Henry Simpson, Subject: Computerized Production of ALFGROW.

Following your approval of my suggestion of February 20, I wrote to KMC Communications[1] Corporation requesting that they send a sales engineer to meet with members of the Administrative[2] Committee to discuss computerization of the manufacture of ALFGROW.

Two series of dates have been[3] suggested: April 17-18 and May 1-2. Which time do you suggest? Perhaps you know of some pending[4] decisions that would involve the members of the committee so that they could not give their best attention to this[5] proposal, which I feel is extremely important to the improvement of our operations. (117)

210▶ Wells and Sawyer, 66 Bridge Street, Bridgeport, Connectict 06630.

Gentlemen: We have been expecting the shipment of casters that your company is subcontracting for us. As[1] you know, the promised date of delivery was November 1. It is now November 5, and the furniture[2] on which these casters is to be used is scheduled for the assembly line on November 10. This means that we[3] must have the shipment by November 14 at the very latest if we are to maintain our flow of operations[4] according to the present route card. Although you told me on the telephone this morning that "the order[5] is practically ready," I am writing to explain our reason for concern.

In the past your company has[6] always been able to meet its delivery timetables, and I feel sure that you are making every effort[7] to sustain your usual record for promptness. On the other hand, you can understand why we are apprehensive[8] about this shipment. Our men and machines are committed to a schedule, and failure to maintain it would mean[9] a great financial loss to NATIONAL PRODUCTS.

Please telephone me immediately if we shall be compelled[10] to revise our schedule. Of course, under the circumstances we shall expect delivery by airfreight at your[11] expense. Also, we should like to revise delivery dates for the remainder of our subcontract by updating[12] them fifteen days. Will this be possible? Sincerely yours, (250)

LESSON 45

212▶ To: All Foremen, Subject: Reordering Raw Materials.

Please remind the stores-record clerks in your department to watch the ordering point for all raw materials. They[1] are to notify the Purchasing Department the day the ordering point is reached, not several days later,[2] as done now in some departments.

Production schedules have been delayed twice this month because the inventory of[3] raw materials was exhausted. This must not happen again if we are to maintain an efficient factory.[4] (80)

213▶ Mr. John P. Hopkins, Missouri Power and Light Company, 2341 Davis Boulevard, St. Louis, Missouri 63125.

Dear Mr. Hopkins: May I express with all sincerity my appreciation for the wonderful job your[1] staff did over the past weekend in repairing the damage done to our powerlines by the ice storm. As you know,[2] the men willingly worked around the clock and did not stop until the job was done. Thus we lost no time in the[3] factory. Both our management and our workmen appreciate this fact.

This performance is in line with your company's[4] tradition of providing service under abnormal conditions.

If there were some way I could personally[5] express my feelings to each man who worked through blizzard conditions day and night, I should certainly like to do[6] so.

Congratulations, Mr. Hopkins, for operating a company that truly renders public service.[7] Sincerely yours, (142)

214▶ Memo to Herbert Schultz, Factory Personnel, Subject: Request for Creation of Security Foreman's Job Classification.

I should like to recommend the establishment of a security foreman's position to become operational[1] on November 1. The primary responsibility of this employee would be the[2] inauguration of the new security precautions outlined in the enclosed memorandum to Mr. Henry[3] Wilson, plant engineer, and approved by him on October 15.

To get the type of employee needed for[4] this assignment, the job should carry a Foreman's 10 or 11 salary classification. After all,[5] if we can reduce pilferage by $50,000 a year through the creation of this job, we shall have[6] saved five times his salary.

We must appoint someone who is trusted implicitly by management and yet has[7] the confidence of the men in the plant. One of the problems in appointing this foreman is the requirement contained[8] in our union contract that all vacancies must be advertised on our company bulletin boards. In my[9] opinion, the particular qualifications for this new position should be sought by management. When we[10] are ready to make an appointment, we can post our recommendation. With the favorable climate now[11] prevailing in the factory, I believe the men will accept this procedure. (234)

215▶ All-State Mail Order Company, 711 Bay Bridge Drive, San Francisco, California 94133.

Gentlemen: We have your letter of August 12, telling us of your plan to keep your electric mixers off the[1] market until you exhaust your supply of the old model. As we are manufacturing these mixers for you,[2] you ask that we store them in our warehouses until you need them.

Unfortunately, we cannot do this, for we[3] simply do not have the room. Our facilities are taxed to the limit by our own goods, and we must move all job[4] lots along to the purchaser just as soon as they are completed.

We realize that this decision will increase[5] your transportation costs, and we wish that we could accommodate you; but this is not possible. I am sure[6] that you will understand our refusal, now that you know the reasons, and that we shall receive your shipping instructions[7] by August 30, when the entire run will be completed. Yours very truly, (156)

Unit 10————————

Secretarial Assignment

1 When confronted with the market analysis, the account executive chose to modify the advertising copy.
2 He led a busy life, attending to numerous community projects.
3 The biannual report was prepared in July and in January.
4 The Better Business Bureau supports the principle that misrepresentations of products are not legally acceptable.
5 The new employee should have followed his supervisor's advice.
6 Can the supervisor effect a change in employees' attitudes?
7 The customer's complaint was respectfully called to the attention of the general manager.
8 The town council met to consider the company's petition for a zoning change.
9 The younger management

personnel chose to lead the revolt against the policies outlined by the Administrative Committee.

10 The principal speaker argued that requirements contracts are not always illegal.

11 The minutes of the sales promotion meeting were respectfully submitted by the sales manager's secretary.

12 He decided to seek legal counsel before attempting to respond to the Federal Trade Commission's inquiry.

13 This decision will affect our production and may result in an inferior product.

14 Six of the twelve people questioned were asked to choose the color of fabric they preferred.

15 Did his supervisor's advice have any effect on his behavior?

16 A biennial sales meeting has been recommended by the marketing director.

LESSON 46

1 Phyllis asked for an appointment with the personnel director; her co-worker did not.

2 We found your advertisement interesting; moreover, we expect to place an order.

3 I believe, however, that we should approve the new budget.

4 We finished ahead of schedule; nevertheless, we were still behind with orders.

5 We believe, furthermore, that other changes should be made in the model.

6 After Friday, March 5, the price goes up; but the increase is small.

7 Many decisions still have to be made; nevertheless, we hope to meet the deadline.

8 We appreciate customer suggestions; furthermore, we often adopt them.

9 I will come Monday; however, don't make special arrangements for me.

10 The trend, however, is to use fewer commas; nevertheless, we should be thoroughly familiar with the rules.

11 After all, the cost is prohibitive; and the benefits would not justify the expenditure.

12 I am convinced that we should proceed with our advertising plans; we must not let our competitors run away with sales.

13 We should investigate current market needs; otherwise, we may produce a product that will encounter customer resistance.

216▶ Mr. Willis P. Hall, Customer Consultant, Rice Hotel, Houston, Texas 77017.

Dear Willis: As product specialist in the sales and installation of our Humbolt electric motors, you will[1] be interested in the enclosed advertising schedule recently planned for the new CR475 series.[2] You will, of course, quickly spot our emphasis on the potential market in the fast-growing Southwest. I know[3] that this is what you have been asking for and that you will be delighted with the sales opportunities this[4] advertising schedule affords.

Please notice that the major

amount of advertising will appear within the[5] next two months. Brochures will be sent to 5,000 prospects in the sales territory. In order to reap the full[6] effect of this direct-mail effort, you may wish to preplan your sales campaign and rough out your proposed itinerary.[7]

A copy of this letter is being sent to your sales manager, Ralph Akin. He will probably contact[8] you shortly in order to discuss an idea he has for inducing those exposed to our brochures to[9] inquire about the CR475 series. One final thought, Willis. If the advertising campaign pays off[10] according to expectations, it will be necessary to arrange for some temporary engineering[11] assistance. Sincerely yours, (223)

217▶ Mr. Henry M. Simpson, President, National Products, Inc., 211 Forest Avenue, St. Louis, Missouri 63100.

Dear Mr. Simpson: Attached is my report on National Products radio advertising policy that[1] you requested in your letter of May 9. As you read the report, undoubtedly you will be (as I was) surprised[2] to see that the facts point so clearly to one decision — the advisability of using local spot[3] advertising for our products rather than network coverage.

Perhaps you will want further data on costs. It's[4] true that the recommended plan will cost a bit more initially than we had estimated during our first[5] discussions; however, the long-range objectives have been ex-

panded.

You were farsighted when you encouraged me[6] to make this comparison study. In a rather convincing fashion, the findings indicate that radio[7] is an excellent medium for territorial selectivity. Since territorial coverage[8] is well defined for most stations, we can select only those stations that broadcast into the areas that we[9] wish to reach. Sincerely yours, (185)

218▶ Burton and Dodson Advertising Agency, 3244 Sutter Avenue, San Francisco, California 94144, Attention Mr. Kent C. Thomas.

Gentlemen: Our Administrative Committee has discussed your advertising Exhibits A, B, and C for our[1] new aerosol containers. It approved Exhibits B and C but has reservations about Exhibit A.[2]

Frankly, we are apprehensive about using such a nonconventional advertisement for the new product[3] in a business weekly that focuses on a most conservative audience. The Committee, however, has[4] made a suggestion that we hope will be acceptable to you.

Why not use Exhibits B and C in *Newsweek*[5] on October 1 and 29? Then we could run Exhibit A on a trial basis on October 22.[6] If the inquiries are keyed to the date of the issue that prompts them, we can thus test the pulling power[7] of your new presentation against the already-proved campaign represented in Exhibits B and C.

We[8] will check the responses

very carefully. If, as you think, the new advertisement proves successful, you may be[9] sure that we shall be receptive to your suggestions for changes in the campaign. At this moment, though, we feel that[10] tests are necessary before such a radically different sales-promotion technique is endorsed. Sincerely[11] yours, (221)

LESSON 47

219▶ Dependable Mailing Lists, Inc., 380 Park Avenue South, New York, New York 10021.

Gentlemen: We should like to purchase a mailing list of retailers of household appliances doing a business[1] in excess of $100,000 a year. Before doing so, however, we have several questions[2] we should like to ask about such a list:

1. When was your list last updated? By what means?

2. Are the retailers[3] on your list classified by volume of business, so that the $100,000 category is separated[4] from the smaller companies?

3. Do you have facilities for the direct mailing of advertising[5] material to the retailers on the list? Our mailings would include sales letters, circulars, pamphlets, booklets,[6] folders, and our 112-page catalog.

4. Could such mailings be extended throughout the entire year to[7] conform to a carefully planned schedule?

We shall await your reply with great interest, for we are anxious to[8] obtain the best possible source of prospective customers. Yours very truly, (174)

220▶ Fortune Magazine, 540 North Michigan Avenue, Chicago, Illinois 60611.

Gentlemen: Thank you for sending us the proof of the short announcement of our new process for developing heat-proof[1] glass that will appear in "Production and Processes" in the August issue of Fortune. I have made a minor[2] correction on the copy, which is enclosed.

Although you provide tear sheets from your magazine to those requesting[3] them, we should like to arrange for a wider distribution of this description. Would it be possible to[4] purchase 10,000 reprints for our own distribution? How much would they cost? How soon would they be available[5] after the appearance of the August issue?

We feel that having your magazine publicize this important[6] development in the manufacture of glass is a real feather in our cap. We appreciate this[7] recognition immensely. Cordially yours, (147)

221▶ To: Arthur C. Williamson, Public Information Director, Subject: Fortune Magazine Report on Heat-Proof Glass.

Here is the page proof of the report on heat-proof glass that is to appear in the August issue of Fortune. In[1] my opinion, the report is sufficiently detailed in its coverage; yet it is not too technical. I have[2] noted one minor correction in the copy that you may wish to make.

Congratulations, Arthur, to you and[3] your staff for a job well done. Your resourcefulness in obtaining publicity of this caliber for a National[4] Products process is exemplary. You can be sure that those of us in advertising and sales appreciate[5] the support you provide. (106)

222▸ The Acme Printing Company, 345 Hudson Street, Champaign, Illinois 61820.

Gentlemen: Paged copy for the eight-page direct-mail brochure announcing our new line of garden tools is enclosed.[1] To confirm our telephone conversation concerning the printing specifications for this job, I am repeating[2] them here.

The page trim is to be $8\frac{1}{2}$ by $3\frac{3}{4}$ inches, so that it will fit into[3] a No. 10 envelope. The text is to be set in 11-point Baskerville type, leaded 1 point. All[4] display heads are to be set in 24-point Nicolas Cochin type. The six line drawings are to be printed[5] in two colors and bled at the margins.

Inasmuch as the copy is typed on a line-for-line basis with illustration[6] space noted, you may wish to give us page proof rather than galley proof. In any event, we must have[7] vandykes by October 15 in order to be reasonably sure of delivery of the completed[8] brochures by November 1. After you have had an opportunity to inspect the copy, would you let me[9] know whether an earlier delivery date would be possible.

If you have any questions about the printing[10] instructions, please telephone me at 572-3244, Extension 267. Sincerely yours,[11] (220)

* * *

▸ Carefully proofread all transcribed material while it is still in your typewriter. Correct any typing errors you may find, and read through the copy to make sure that it makes sense. Refer to your shorthand notes to verify quickly prices and dates that you have transcribed. The copy should be removed from the machine only when you are sure the material is free from all errors.

LESSON 48

223▸ Burton and Dodson Advertising Agency, 3244 Sutter Avenue, San Francisco, California 94144.

Gentlemen: Please submit another logotype design using words Dust-Away—a new product of NATIONAL[1] PRODUCTS, INC., St. Louis, Missouri. Use Futura Medium Condensed typeface. Rush to meet October[2] 10 closing for Ladies' Home Journal. Sincerely yours, (50)

224▸ Girl Scouts of the USA, 830 Third Avenue, New York, New York 10022.

Ladies: Your letter asking us to include a reminder about support of the Girl Scouts' annual drive for[1] funds in all advertising during the month of November has been received.

Although we have a budget

allotment[2] for institutional advertising, we also have a policy that requires changing the recipient[3] of such space annually. You will remember that last year we gave you a boxed-in announcement in all our[4] full-page advertisements appearing in national magazines during November. Thus, our policy requires[5] us to decline your request this year so that we can assist ánother organization in its annual[6] fund drive.

We do have a number of worthy requests each year, and we hope that you will approve of our method of[7] sharing a limited amount of help with more than one youth organization.

Best wishes to you in this year's[8] fund drive. Girl Scouts certainly deserve the support of every community in the United States. Sincerely[9] yours, (181)

225▶ The Reuben H. Donnelly Company, 420 LaSalle Street, Chicago, Illinois 60610.

Gentlemen: Will it be possible to contract with you for national advertising in all Yellow Pages[1] in cities having a population of over 250,000? We should like to insert an[2] advertisement $2\frac{1}{2}$ inches by 2 inches under NATIONAL PRODUCTS. The copy would describe the products[3] and name the local distributor or distributors. A benday treatment of our company insignia[4] would be included.

If we place these advertisements through your company instead of through the local telephone[5] companies, what dis-

count rate would we get?

Is production of various issues of the Yellow Pages staggered[6] throughout the year? Can you now give us the schedule for submitting copy for each city?

We are very anxious to[7] place this advertising through your central agency rather than through local representatives. We could thus save[8] time and achieve a uniformity that would improve our national image. Yours very truly, (178)

226▶ To: Mr. Henry M. Simpson, President, Subject: Advertising Media.

Printers' Ink has just published the following figures about the distribution of advertising expenditures[1] among the various media that will, I believe, interest you. They may well influence our thinking[2] about next year's budget.

Newspapers, 31.0; Direct Mail, 14.9; Television, 14.2;[3] Magazines, 7.9; Radio, 5.8; Business Papers, 4.9; Outdoor, 1.4; Miscellaneous,[4] 19.9; Total, 100.0.

The increasingly large proportion of advertising expenditure[5] going to television is significant. It suggests to me that we may be wise if we raise our last[6] year's figure of 8 percent to conform more nearly to the national average. Our percentage for direct[7] mail is now only 10 percent, almost 5 percent below the national average. Proposed further[8] increases in postal rates, however, may induce reluctance to move more heavily into the direct-mail field.[9]

If these figures suggest any

ideas that would help me in estimating next year's advertising expenditures,[10] I should appreciate your sharing them with me. (210)

227▸ McGill Advertising Company, 416 South Wabash Avenue, Chicago, Illinois 60605.

Gentlemen: We are interested in having your agency develop a French-fold brochure in three colors[1] to introduce our new electric percolator to consumers. I am enclosing specifications[2] for the percolator and illustrations so that you can prepare preliminary sketches and dummies that[3] we can discuss when I am in Chicago on September 19.

Enclosed also are several brochures that[4] have recently come to my desk that seem to have the kind of appeal we are seeking. The one from Lanham KitchenWares[5] is especially attractive, I think. Has some new process been used to give such an attractive sheen to the[6] illustration? The copy, too, seems outstanding.

We hope to keep the weight of this piece of direct mail down to 2[7] ounces and thus save on postage. We also want it designed to fit No. 10 envelopes so that it can be[8] used as an enclosure with other mail sent out by our distributors to their customers. Yours truly, (178)

LESSON 49

232▸ Chicago Rapid Transit System, 403 State Street, Chicago, Illinois 60610.

Gentlemen: We have recently signed a contract with you for the display of 1,000 car cards advertising[1] NATIONAL PRODUCTS electric toasters during the months of September and October.

A small but important[2] point has been overlooked in our agreement. Our campaign would lose much of its effectiveness if any cards that[3] are marred in any way remain on display. May we, then, have your assurance that your car cleaners and inspectors[4] will be instructed to replace any worn NATIONAL PRODUCTS cards when preparing the cars for service? Yours cordially,[5] (100)

233▸ Middle-Western Printers, 514 Oak Street, Bloomington, Indiana 47401.

Gentlemen: Your second printing of our spring catalog does not seem to meet the standards of the first printing. The ink[1] on some of the pages containing illustrations has offset on adjoining pages.

Although I am not[2] a great authority on printing, I wonder why this happened. Perhaps the paper stock we are using is too[3] highly glazed for adequate ink absorption.

Do you think that it would be wise to change the stock to a paper having[4] less surface sizing? Do you have samples that you might suggest?

If so, please run the copy for a typical[5] page (such as page 119) on several qualities and send me samples along with your recommendations. Even[6] if there is an additional charge for the new paper, we should be glad to share the costs. I know from past[7] experience with Middle-Western Printers that your concern with quality is as great as ours. Yours truly,[8] (160)

234▶ To: Fred R. Hart.

I agree with you completely on your timing of the newspaper announcement of the new factory to be[1] built in Gary. It is best to withhold any release until all plans have been approved by management, which[2] I would guess might be July 1. As you know, there is still some question as to whether we should build on the River[3] Road site or elsewhere; even the plans for the building itself have undergone several changes in the past two[4] weeks.

I shall keep you informed. In the meantime, I should welcome your suggestions on the preparation of the news[5] release. The Daily News has expressed its willingness to print the entire story when we are ready. (118)

235▶ To: Ralph C. Akin, Sales Manager, Subject: March 7 Advertisement in The Farm Journal.

As you know, our full-page advertisement of ALFGROW appeared in the March 7 issue of The Farm Journal. This advertisement[1] was keyed by requesting that all inquiries be addressed to Department M.

You will be delighted with[2]

the pulling power of this advertisement. We have already received 477 inquiries,[3] which have been routed to the salesmen in the territories involved. Thirty-five of these inquiries were received[4] from representatives of government agencies involved with agricultural projects in developing[5] countries. Ten inquiries were received from foreign governments or distributors to foreign markets.

It appears,[6] Ralph, that The Farm Journal is our best medium for advertising ALFGROW. (134)

LESSON 50

239▶ Burton and Dodson Advertising Agency, 3244 Sutter Avenue, San Francisco, California 94144.

Gentlemen: We have reviewed the ideas for front-page copy as recorded in your Conference Report No.[1] 127, dated February 16.

Frankly, I don't feel that any one of the six possible headline[2] ideas that we developed in the conference conveys exactly what we want to highlight about the output[3] of our Elmira packaging plant. I think that the headline we choose should emphasize our entry into the[4] aerosol-container field and yet convey the idea that metal cans are not completely outdated.

Did[5] you see the Modern Packaging Company's advertisement last week in *U. S. News and World Report?*[6] I thought it captured the happy blending of the old and the new.

I now have two ideas to suggest. We might[7] change Suggestion 3 to include the subhead, "Along with our metal cans that package many of the world's finest[8] foods." We might show a montage of famous brands of foods in modern packaging with the caption, "Choose your packaging[9] — either old or new — to create demand for your product."

If either of these ideas appeals to you, perhaps[10] you will sketch a layout around the one that has the greater sales appeal. Let me know which you choose, and I will supply[11] basic copy information. Yours very truly, (230)

240▶ Mr. Kent C. Thomas, Burton and Dodson Advertising Agency, 3244 Sutter Avenue, San Francisco, California 94144.

Dear Mr. Thomas: You have our unequivocal approval of the final changes made in the Dust-Away[1] newspaper mats. In our opinion, the revised copy will get our message to the metropolitan community.[2]

You are hereby authorized to release this advertisement so that it will appear in the magazine section[3] of the Sunday edition of the Boston Herald.

I should like to congratulate you on the excellent[4] job your company has done on this advertisement. I am sure that it will prove to be one of the most successful[5] that we have ever had. Sincerely yours, (108)

241▶ Atlantic Printers, 430 Olive Street, St. Louis, Missouri 63166.

Gentlemen: On Tuesday we received the 25,000 envelope stuffers that you recently printed for[1] us. Unfortunately, however, we must reject the entire shipment. Apparently your folding machine was not[2] operating properly, for practically the entire shipment is folded so inaccurately that[3] we should not wish to distribute the stuffers to our dealers for enclosure with monthly bills.

We have done business[4] with your company for many years, and we are disappointed that the quality of this job makes it necessary[5] to ask for a credit memorandum for the entire job. On the other hand, we know that your usual[6] standards of quality will cause you to agree with us that we cannot accept this order.

Confirming our[7] telephone conversation this morning, I am asking that you pick up the shipment at our headquarters this week.[8] Sincerely yours, (162)

* * *

▶ Use a red pencil to "flag" your notes when taking dictation. These notations can be spotted quickly when you begin to transcribe.

Unit 11————————

Secretarial Assignment

1 For some time I have used that brand of soap.
2 The lace trim complements the fabric well.

3 We believe success is imminent with our new product.

4 Here are the frames as well as the hooks therefor.

5 We had already made the decision; therefore, there is no choice.

6 The members of the committee are all ready to submit a report.

7 I hope sometime to spend some time in Europe.

8 Some time should be spent every day in planning one's work.

9 Bankruptcy has seemed imminent for some time.

10 Sometimes a well-deserved compliment is neglected.

11 We hope to get their order; therefore, we approve the trip.

12 The invoice is for $71.87, and here is payment therefor.

13 I have felt for some time that we should manufacture a new line to complement our present offerings.

14 The advertising was already prepared for the new engines.

15 The advertising is all ready for the television presentation.

16 Eminent people are often complimented for their services.

LESSON 51

1 The preestablished rate will be used in computing the tariff.

2 One hundred twenty-five people can be seated in the room.

3 We will reenter the plastics market in the fall.

4 We intend to de-emphasize the safety factor in our next advertising campaign.

5 We plan to travel on a toll-less route on our trans-Canadian trip.

6 This shell-like pattern will be used in the newly designed fabric.

7 Anti-imperialistic propaganda was expressed again and again at the conclave.

8 Seventy-five votes against the proposition were enough to defeat it.

9 The inter-American trade conference was most successful.

10 The property contains seventy-five acres.

11 We have a Desk-Fax for sending telegrams directly from the office.

12 We seek the cooperation of all companies interested in raising quality standards.

13 Mr. Williams was appointed to coordinate the work of five divisions.

14 He was not told that the format had been preestablished.

242▸ Mr. Mark M. Gibson, Rice Hotel, Houston, Texas 77004, Hold for Arrival on May 27.

Dear Mark: Sam Collins, our sales engineer in the Southwest, will be in Houston on June 11 and 12 on a[1] special assignment to estimate a possible food-conveyor installation at the medical center.[2] If you have other prospects for custom-built National Products, we could schedule Sam for your territory for[3] the remainder of the week (June 13 through 15).

You stated in your April report that you had received[4] inquiries from the Shamrock Hotel, Hodges and Smith, and the Pinnacle Supermarket in the Houston area[5] and from Peterson Oil Transport in Galveston. You may wish to follow up on these leads and if possible develop[6] other prospects in the two weeks remaining before Sam's visit.

Please let me know by June 2 whether[7] you have been able to arrange a sufficient number of sales consultations to justify our keeping Sam[8] in the area for three additional days. Sincerely yours, (172)

243▶ To: All Salesmen, Subject: Long Distance Telephone Selling.

National Products recently purchased WATS (Wide Area Toll Service), covering all six bands into[1] which the continental United States is divided. Unlimited telephone service is now available[2] for a flat rate, without separate long distance tolls.

This new and improved communication system will[3] enable the Sales Department to communicate more effectively and to provide better customer service.[4]

The following suggestions are offered as guidelines for improving our long distance telephone procedures.[5]

1. Maintain a time schedule indicating when an established customer might possibly be ready to reorder[6] items you have sold him. A personal visit may not be necessary; a telephone call may be all[7] a customer needs to replenish his supply.

2. Telephone ahead for an appointment with a prospective[8] customer. Doing this regularly will enable you to service more territory in less time.

3.[9] Telephone customers on special occasions, such as the opening of a new branch, the day his purchases reach[10] a certain high level, or the day his store gets unusual publicity.

4. Encourage customers to[11] telephone you and reverse the charges when deliveries are delayed, terms cannot be met, or merchandise is[12] defective.

5. Telephone prospective customers if a sales engineer or a special demonstrator is[13] scheduled to be in your territory and is available to call on them.

6. Telephone the headquarters[14] office to discuss any special problem.

7. When telephoning long distance, preplan your conversation. Get[15] to the business at hand as soon as you can.

Lest you forget, an admonition may be in order. Try not to[16] abuse the telephone privilege. During the initial stages of WATS, calls will be monitored.[17] Employees found using the service for personal calls or talking for unreasonably long periods will be[18] asked to pay for such calls. Flagrant misuse of the service will result in the loss of the unlimited telephone[19] call privilege.

Until further notice, please include an account of your use of WATS service in[20] your weekly report. (403)

244▶ Mr. Walter C. Forbes, Re-

gional Sales Manager, National Products, Inc., 725 Buena Vista Drive, Raleigh, North Carolina 27638.

Dear Walt: It will be possible for us to supply the backdrop and complete setting for your display of National[1] Products garden tools at the Winston-Salem annual garden show.

A cardboard template is enclosed to show[2] you how to assemble the display. Although garden tools are not a part of this display assembly, you can obtain[3] them from your customers. The display will be sent by express to the site of the garden show; it should arrive[4] on Friday, March 6, in plenty of time for the opening of the show on Saturday. Sincerely yours, (98)

LESSON 52

245▶ To: Stuart P. Henderson, Manager of Advertising Department, Subject: Tie-in with "Home in Suburbia."

Frankly, Stuart, I am not enthusiastic about your suggestion to tie in our promotion of patio[1] furniture with the premiere of the movie "Home in Suburbia." The proposal is clever but, in my[2] opinion, impractical. A display of the furniture in the lobby of every first-run theater would require[3] an unjustifiable expenditure of budgeted funds. Furthermore, most theater lobbies are not[4] sufficiently protected. The risk of possible damage due to carelessness and to vandalism

would be too[5] great. (101)

246▶ Mr. Benjamin J. Carter, 4123 Euclid Avenue, Cleveland, Ohio 44125.

Dear Ben: The enclosed letter has been reproduced on our automatic typewriter and mailed to Mr. Beatty.[1] As you requested, we have also personalized and mailed this sales letter to the other 24 customers[2] you expect to call on next week.

This promotion should bring you a substantial increase in lawn mower sales. I[3] will be watching the results. Yours cordially, (68)

247▶ Mr. Harmon R. Beatty, Beatty Hardware Store, 222 Davis Boulevard, Bowling Green, Ohio 43402.

Dear Mr. Beatty: When you demonstrate a CUTCLOSE lawn mower with its streamlined design and cutting-clipping[1] combination, more often than not you have a quick sale, a satisfied customer, and $13.25[2] profit.

Men, women, and boys like the CUTCLOSE. Men like it because it cuts right up to walls, fences, trees, and borders.[3] They don't have to spend extra time clipping the edges. They like its sturdy construction and its drive shaft mounted[4] on free-rolling, permanently lubricated, sealed ball bearings that won't rust. They like its self-sharpening blades.

Women[5] like it because they push only 8¼ pounds when they cut the grass. They like it, too, because they can[6] adjust the handle to the cutting height they want without bending down; with just a flick of the hand, the cutting height[7] is regulated.

Junior likes it, too. He knows that he can cut a clean, even 16-inch swath every trip[8] across the lawn. His chores are finished in a jiffy, and he is off to the swimming pool or to the pitcher's mound.[9]

No doubt many of your customers have been reading about the CUTCLOSE in the full-page, four-color ads now [10] appearing in Life. Perhaps you will want to post the enclosed reprints in your windows. Note the generous terms for[11] servicing the CUTCLOSE.

In these days of inflation, the $42.95 retail price of the CUT-CLOSE[12] will appeal to your customers. Our price to you, including shipping charges, is $29.70.[13]

Your NATIONAL PRODUCTS salesman, Ben Carter, will be in Bowling Green next week. He can write your order then[14] so that you will be sure to have CUTCLOSE lawn mowers on hand when your customers begin asking for them next month.[15] You can expect immediate delivery. Yours cordially, (312)

248▶ To: Henry P. Walters, Vice-President, Subject: Computer Control of Marketing.

Have you read the article in the April 17 issue of Business Week titled "The Computer's Newest[1] Conquest: Marketing"?

Although National Products is using electronic data processing successfully[2] in inventory control, much needs to be done to help us in analyzing our computer output. For the[3] most part, this article discusses the daily analysis of retail sales; however, I believe that we[4] could make the same applications to sales to distributors.

May I discuss the implications with you after[5] you have read the report? (105)

249▶ Plattsburgh Retail Center, 390 North Margaret Street, Plattsburgh, New York 12902.

Gentlemen: Mr. Ben Huntington has been assigned to the territory formerly covered by our salesman,[1] Mr. Frank Harding, who has become eastern sales manager.

Mr. Huntington has represented NATIONAL[2] PRODUCTS for the past five years in West Virginia. He is thoroughly familiar with our lines and our standards for[3] customer service; so I am sure that he can help you with not only the choice of goods that will meet your needs but also[4] with merchandising suggestions.

We want to thank you for the many courtesies you showed Mr. Harding during[5] the seven years he called on you. Yours very cordially, (110)

LESSON 53

250▶ To: Henry Miller, Sales Engineer; Harry Nelson, Sales Engineer; Abe Olsten, Sales Engineer; Ben Phillips, Sales Engineer; Walter Reston, Sales Engi-

neer; Jim Summers, Sales Engineer, Subject: Training Session.

Please arrange your schedules so that you can attend an emergency three-day briefing session at headquarters on[1] March 17 through 19 on Product 83.

The meeting will be held in the laboratories by Dr.[2] Millard C. Egan of R and D.

As you know, Product 83 has not performed satisfactorily. We[3] are told that the difficulty lies in certain precision features that are not properly adjusted during[4] installation.

Although we realize that you are getting short notice on this meeting, we feel that the reputation[5] of National Products rests on eliminating any problems that our customers may experience.[6] Therefore, this meeting must take precedence over regular schedules.

Reservations have been made for all of[7] you at the Chase Hotel for March 16 through 18. If you plan to spend additional time in the R and D laboratories[8] while you are in St. Louis, we shall be glad to change your reservations to suit your plans. (177)

251▶ To: Regional Sales Managers, Subject: Speed-up in Filling Orders.

The salesmen under your supervision send their orders directly to their district office, which transmits them to[1] headquarters. Every week we accumulate the total sales for each district and send you a report

that is[2] expected to reach you on Tuesday.

On March 4 we introduced a shipping procedure that will speed orders[3] to our customers. Every day our data-processing equipment at National headquarters classifies[4] orders according to the shipping center that will fill the order for each product. For instance, all orders[5] to be filled from Kansas City are relayed to that point electronically and filled immediately.[6]

We anticipate that improved delivery service will increase sales appreciably. We want you to have the privilege[7] of telling your salesmen of this speed-up in service. (151)

252▶ To: All Salesmen, Subject: Holiday Promotion of Home Appliances.

October is, of course, your best month. National Products wants to make this October and the rest of the holiday[1] buying season better than ever.

We are ready to ship your customers selling aids that could cause them to[2] double their orders for holiday goods.

As you know, the theme of our Christmas promotions is "Make This a Home-Appliance[3] Christmas." We have prepared four brochures for distribution by retailers stocking National appliances:[4]

Who Said an Electric Iron Can't Be Glamorous?

Would She Prefer a Garbage Disposal to a Fur Jacket?[5]

Shaving Made Modern.

For Rainy-Day Laundry.

Samples of all four brochures are enclosed. When you call on your prospects[6] during the rest of September and all of October, offer them copies of any or all of these brochures[7] for use as envelope stuffers to be sent with monthly bills or as counter handouts. Show them, too, the enclosed four advertising mats that are[8] available for promoting National appliances in local newspapers. Then be sure to tell them to[9] include the number of mats as well as brochures that they want.

When you send in your orders, be sure to include the[10] number of brochures requested by each customer. The brochures are already wrapped in 100-copy lots[11] for shipping just as soon as you supply the addresses. (230)

253▶ Dr. Franklin Miller, Chairman of the Accounting Department, Miller College, Front Street at Brown Boulevard, Denver, Colorado 80205.

My dear Doctor Miller: On June 13, 1965, our salesman, Jim Murtha, sold your college five new NATIONAL[1] electronic calculators for use in the Accounting Department. As you know, these machines were guaranteed[2] for one year.

That year has now expired. Because we want you to continue to have the fine repair service you have[3] enjoyed this past year, we have recently introduced a yearly service contract on these machines.

For an annual[4] rate of $25 for each machine, our service en-

gineers will answer any emergency call[5] promptly and get the calculator back into use quickly. In addition, they will come to Miller College and[6] give each machine a routine check and thorough cleaning every three months during the year. There will never be any[7] additional charges for service, no matter how many times the service engineer may repair your machines.[8] The only possible expense to you would be for replacement of needed machine parts.

Why not write or call[9] us today and say, "Put the Miller College Accounting Department down for your comprehensive yearly service[10] plan for our five NATIONAL calculators." We think you will be glad you did; for in today's competitive market[11] in the educational field, the reputation of an accounting program depends on the availability[12] and the good working condition of the modern equipment actually used in business. Yours truly,[13] (260)

LESSON 54

258▶ Mr. Edwin C. Leighton, Brown Palace Hotel, Denver, Colorado 80202.

Dear Ed: I have just had a conference with Harold C. Poling, our credit manager, about our relations[1] with the Reliable Mercantile Company, of Pueblo, Colorado. As you know, you sold this store[2] $437.71 worth of goods on May 14.

On its April 27 weekly[3] report of poor risks, however, our Credit Department listed the Reliable Mercantile Company[4] as being 60 days delinquent in payment of Invoice 411 for $134.67.[5] As you know, this list is sent to all salesmen with the understanding that they must not accept further[6] orders from any customers appearing on it unless they have cleared the credit status of the account[7] with the Credit Department. Mr. Poling says you have not done this.

The order has, of course, been refused, as this[8] customer has never answered any of several collection letters. Will you please make a special call on[9] the Reliable Mercantile Company to see whether you can facilitate the collection of this account.[10] Telephone me the results of your visit.

In the meantime, Ed, please observe the rules under which salesmen must[11] operate. To accept an order from an unsatisfactory credit risk places your company in an[12] embarrassing situation with both the customer and the salesman, who must lose his commission on the sale.[13] Yours cordially, (262)

259▶ Mr. Fred Zimmerman, Connor Hotel, Third and Grand, Laramie, Wyoming 82070.

Dear Fred: Your November orders fell off 10 percent over the corresponding month last year. It occurs to[1] me that our company policy to adopt the use of WATS may be the reason, and I should like your[2] frank evaluation of the effect of this move in your case.

I am especially interested in your[3] reaction because you are in the most sparsely populated territory of any salesman in the company.[4] Perhaps your customers miss the friendly relationship you can establish through a personal visit.[5] Possibly they resent long distance telephone calls.

Although the overall effect of the new policy has[6] been to reduce travel expense by 53 percent at the same time that we have reduced net sales by only[7] 2 percent, we do not want to hamper any salesman by arbitrary rules. Just tell me whether you can[8] sell effectively under the new system. Make any suggestions that you feel would improve our selling in Wyoming.[9] Yours very truly, (184)

260▶ Mr. Harold L. Carney, District Sales Manager, National Products, Inc., 433 Walnut Street, Salt Lake City, Utah 84118.

Dear Harold: Here is a copy of a letter to Ed Leighton that is self-explanatory. His continued[1] disregard for the monthly list of delinquent accounts disturbs me greatly. This is his third order in a month[2] from a customer without a satisfactory credit rating.

Both Harold Poling and I think you should see[3] him and talk with him about his repeated disregard of company regulations. Apparently, he feels[4] that making a sale is the most important thing, whether National Products is ever paid or not.

We hope that[5] you will be

able to make Ed see the necessity for conforming to company policy; otherwise,[6] we feel it will be necessary to let him go.

If anybody can get us out of this sticky situation,[7] you can. Good luck. Yours cordially, (148)

LESSON 55

263▸ Lumsden Knitting Mills, Old Fort Road, Asheville, North Carolina 28800, Attention: Mr. Abraham C. Lumsden, Purchasing Agent.

Gentlemen: Mr. Roy L. Brennan, our representative in North Carolina, has reported that you plan[1] to cancel your contract for pliofilm bags that you use to package the sweaters that you manufacture. He[2] indicated that you were dissatisfied with the way we have been servicing your account.

Needless to say, we did[3] not have prior knowledge of your feelings. I hope your decision is not irrevocable. Mr. Walter[4] C. Forbes, our regional sales manager, and I should like to work out an agreement that would resolve any problems[5] that now exist.

At that time we should like to show you the new pliofilm bag with a self-seal feature that will[6] protect a sweater no matter how many times it is removed and reinserted into the bag. Your advertising[7] could stress this permanent storage feature. For this new line, we are increasing the range of sizes.

We can[8] meet with you in Asheville on February 17 and

should like to have lunch with you. Mr. Brennan is being[9] transferred to our West Coast region. If his replacement has been chosen before our proposed visit, we shall ask him[10] to join us for lunch.

Would you telephone me collect if you cannot meet with us at that time. Sincerely yours, (218)

264▸ Mr. Jack Bowman, Shamrock Hotel, 2712 Oak Springs Drive, Houston, Texas 77015.

Dear Jack: A copy of my letter preparing the way for your visit to Martin Food Processors in Corpus[1] Christi the first week in January is enclosed. This company sent for a copy of "Let Your Packaging[2] Sell Your Products," which was advertised in the December 7 issue of the bulletin of the National[3] Association of Food Chains. A photocopy of the request is also enclosed.

Since their letter[4] indicates an interest in redesigning the packages in which present products are now being sold, I suggest[5] that you demonstrate two products:

1. Our new sealed plastic package for precooked vegetables, which can be immersed[6] in hot water and boiled for twenty minutes.

2. Our aluminum container for ONE DINNER OR TWO, which can[7] be separated into two individual pans if only one meal is being prepared.

Although my letter[8] refers only to the new vegetable bag, I suggest that you also be pre-

95

pared to explore the possibility[9] of selling exclusive rights to our ONE DINNER OR TWO. Martin Food Processors have marketed such[10] frozen foods as baked chicken, roast-beef hash, and baked macaroni and cheese for several years and may welcome the[11] introduction of such a novel idea. (229)

265▶ Memo to Stuart Henderson, Manager, Advertising Department, Subject: Reprint of "Let Your Packaging Sell Your Products."

The immediate success of the booklet "Let Your Packaging Sell Your Products" has been phenomenal. We have[1] had about twenty requests a day from our offer of this brochure to interested frozen-food processors[2] in the December 7 issue of the bulletin of the National Association of Food Chains. Our[3] salesmen tell me that they find that it supports their presentations as they meet with prospective customers. It has[4] undoubtedly contributed to the 12 percent increase in sales in our packaging unit during the three-month[5] period covering October, November, and December.

Although we realize that we have exhausted[6] our budget for the issuance of this brochure, we should like to request that a reprint of 2,000[7] additional copies be authorized immediately. We feel that its popularity could not have been foreseen[8] when we first planned this publication. (167)

266▶ Mr. Walter C. Forbes, 725 Buena Vista Drive, Raleigh, North Carolina 27600.

Dear Walter: The enclosed letter is self-explanatory. I hope that it is not too late to repair the damage[1] that Roy Brennan did to this contract. I am sure that your evaluation of the situation is correct[2] and that we lost out because of his handling of credit terms. Anyway, we are lucky that he is being[3] transferred at just this time.

If Mr. Lumsden will see us, I shall fly to Asheville and meet you there. Perhaps we can[4] swing over to Knoxville by car and try to get the Southern Mills contract on February 18. Do you know[5] of any other accounts that may be in jeopardy because of Brennan's handling of them? Maybe we should[6] call on other customers. Sincerely yours, (127)

Unit 12

Secretarial Assignment

1 How many carats is the diamond in your ring?
2 Insert a caret on the galley to indicate the omission.
3 Columbus was an immigrant to America.
4 Are you averse to that suggestion?
5 Nothing could be further from the truth.
6 Should he proceed when we get an adverse reaction?
7 This step should precede any further negotiation of the contract.

8 Our plant is farther from our source of raw materials than it should be.

9 The immigration quota for certain countries is very restrictive.

10 The bracelet is 14-karat gold.

11 He proceeded to give an adverse report.

LESSON 56

1 He said that he would be in Dallas that morning but would go on to Austin.

2 He said that he would begin work on July 1; but I asked, "Can you start Monday?"

3 "Where," Mr. Simpson asked, "will you be on Friday?"

4 The contract states, "The premises may not be subleased"; otherwise, you could have the property for the summer.

5 Did you include the phrase "during the course of employment"?

6 We sent our employees a bonus with a greeting, "Happy holidays."

7 The speaker exclaimed, "Down with all labor unions!"

8 Why do you say that you dislike personnel work?

9 Who can judge his meaning when he said, "I don't aspire to the presidency"?

10 Invite the following representatives from "middle management": Brown, Henderson, and Rogers.

11 The message stated, "Plane delayed four hours."

12 "What is your beginning salary?" is probably the worst possible approach to an interview.

13 The newspaper report stated: "The new rates will go into effect on May 1."

14 I ask that you delay your decision until after the committee meeting.

15 A pre-Thanksgiving ad stated, "These prices are 25 percent lower than last year's."

267▶ The Miller Mart, 3174 Jefferson Avenue, Davenport, Iowa 52803.

Gentlemen: A duplicate order of Invoice No. 34222 is being rushed to you today[1] by airexpress. It will cover the loss you sustained when the original order was damaged in transit by[2] flood water. We hope that shipping you this merchandise will help you to get back in business promptly.

Although the[3] carrier is not responsible for the loss, which is legally termed "an act of God," we are fortunate that freight[4] charges include insurance. If you will sign the enclosed affidavit attesting to the amount of the loss, we[5] shall recover most of the loss that has been sustained. You will not be billed for the duplicate order.

Our sales[6] manager, Ralph C. Akin, will ask your NATIONAL PRODUCTS salesman to make a special trip to Davenport if[7] you feel that his coming would assist you in this emergency period. Please wire Mr. Akin if you need[8] further help in assembling this new stock of goods. Sincerely yours, (172)

268▶ First National Bank, 433

River Street, Dubuque, Iowa 52001.

Gentlemen: Enclosed is an order bill of lading and sight draft for $345.58,[1] drawn on the Hayes Emporium, 255 Eighth Avenue, Dubuque, Iowa. We have notified them[2] that this shipment of lawn-mower parts will be delivered to their Dubuque warehouse just as soon as they honor the[3] sight draft. The Hayes Emporium's agent can use the endorsed bill of lading as their authority for delivery.[4]

In addition to handling this transaction for us, will you please provide us with an evaluation[5] of the credit standing of this store. We would rather extend credit if possible and thus reduce the inconvenience[6] of using order bills of lading. Sincerely yours, (131)

269▸ Mr. Walter J. James, Manager, Furniture Fixtures, A Division of National Products, Inc., High Point, North Carolina 27260.

Dear Mr. James: I should like to ask you several questions about a proposed plan to reduce costs of shipping[1] furniture to our five regional warehouses from which orders are filled. All furniture currently shipped to our[2] warehouses is received, assembled, and marked "S. U." for purposes of assessing tariffs. We are convinced that[3] it will be possible to reduce rates appreciably if we can ship furniture unassembeld, or knocked down[4] and labeled "K. D." Several important factors need to

be considered, however, before we can make a[5] final decision:

In your opinion, could assembly units be set up in the regional warehouses where[6] knocked-down furniture could be handled efficiently?

Could the quality of our furniture be maintained under[7] this system?

What is your estimate of the cost of maintaining an assembly unit at each warehouse? Your[8] summary information on sales volume will help you in answering this question.

Could our less-expensive lines be[9] shipped unassembled more satisfactorily than our high-quality lines?

After you have given us an[10] opinion and an estimate, we shall know whether to pursue this idea further. Sincerely yours, (218)

270▸ To: Mr. Ralph C. Akin, Sales Manager, Subject: Lumsden Knitting Mills.

Yes, the Lumsden Knitting Mills has a justifiable complaint The packing slip does not conform to the order.[1] It shows that their Purchase Order No. 877 was short 12 dozen boxes of pliofilm bags.

The error[2] was made in our Packing Department and not by the salesman, as you suspected. I have sent the shortage by[3] airexpress today; it should arrive before your next trip to Asheville. (72)

271▸ The J. L. Johnson Farm Products Company, 411 Railroad Street, Wichita, Kansas 67219.

Gentlemen: Your Order No. 875 for a carload lot of fertilizer and chicken feed will be shipped[1] on Friday, October 11, via the M K and T Railroad. Our Invoice No. 8902 and[2] straight bill of lading are enclosed.

Since the order will arrive on Saturday, the car will be placed on your spur track[3] for unloading on Monday. We are notifying you of the expected arrival date well in advance so[4] that you can arrange for the adequate protection of the shipment during the period that will elapse between[5] arrival at destination and unloading. We should warn you that considerable damage has been done[6] recently along the M K and T tracks to carload shipments between arrival time and unloading especially[7] if the order arrives over the weekend.

We want you to know that we appreciate your order, the third[8] in the past three months. We shall try to do everything possible to merit your confidence in NATIONAL[9] PRODUCTS. Yours very truly, (184)

LESSON 57

272▶ To: Helen Marie Brady, Secretary to Mr. Robert L. Simpson, Subject: Reservations to London on April 7.

Mr. Simpson has the choice of two flights — one daytime and the other at night.
TWA Transfer in New York[1]
Leave St. Louis 9:15 a.m.

Arrive New York 12:10 p.m.
Leave New York 2:30 p.m.
Arrive London[2] 2:00 a.m.
TWA Transfer in Chicago
Leave St. Louis 8:20 p.m.
Arrive Chicago[3] 9:10 p.m.
Leave Chicago 11:00 p.m.
Arrive London 12:30 p.m.
If Mr. Simpson will indicate[4] his flight preference, we will make the necessary arrangements to pick up his ticket. (97)

273▶ To: Mr. James M. Walsh, Production Manager, Subject: Water Transportation of Steel.

The cost of shipping steel to St. Louis from the Bessemer mills can be reduced by 15 percent if we bring[1] it by train from Birmingham to Memphis and then transfer it to barges for shipment up the river.

The cost of[2] shipping steel from Birmingham to our Los Angeles plant can be reduced as much as 25 percent by using[3] railway transportation to New Orleans, where it is transferred to ship.

In each instance the transfer of steel[4] shipments from train to barge would lengthen existing shipping schedules. Deliveries of steel to St. Louis would be[5] delayed five days, for example, and deliveries to Los Angeles would be delayed as much as three weeks.

After[6] you have studied your production schedules for the present quarter, please advise me whether or not we should attempt[7] to effect these savings. (145)

274▶ The Mervin Furniture Company, 700 Oak Street, Hastings, Nebraska 68901.

Gentlemen: Your letter of April 8 reported a shortage of two patio chairs in our shipment of March[1] 20. We checked the processing of your order and found that the packing slip shows that the 20 chairs ordered[2] were actually included in your shipment. In addition, the initials of both the packer and the inspector[3] verify the count. Apparently, two chairs were pilfered while the goods were in transit.

Unfortunately,[4] we may have difficulty in collecting from the carrier inasmuch as more than 15 days elapsed[5] before you reported the shortage. In any event, we shall file the claim. Please complete the enclosed affidavit[6] confirming the shortage and return it to us promptly.

In the meantime, do you want us to replace the two missing[7] chairs? If our claim is paid, the duplicate order will not be charged to you, of course. Yours very cordially,[8] (160)

275▶ Claims Department, Union Pacific Railroad, Union Station, St. Louis, Missouri 63100.

Gentlemen: Claim No. 433339. On January 17 we filed the above claim for[1] $45.91 for a shortage in our shipment to Weber and Hayes in Denver, Colorado.[2] All supporting documents were enclosed with the claim.

Although six months have elapsed since the claim was filed, you have not[3] communi-

cated your decision about honoring this obligation.

May we hear from you at once? Sincerely[4] yours, (81)

276▶ Pennsylvania Railroad, Pennsylvania Station, Seventh Avenue at 33 Street, New York, New York 10036, Attention of Freight Department.

Gentlemen: We are assigning our own clerk to prepare waybills to accompany all shipments by PRR.[1] Our reason for undertaking this responsibility rather than leaving it to your agents is that they[2] have recently given instructions as to routes the merchandise is to take between point of origin and[3] destination that have resulted in circuitous routes and unnecessary delays for our customers. We[4] think that our own routing clerk can choose more expeditious and less costly routes. If so, we can save on both inventories[5] and freight charges.

The waybills will be submitted to your agents along with the already-prepared bills[6] of lading when shipments leave our premises. Yours very truly, (172)

277▶ Kennedy, Martin, and Willing, Attorneys at Law, 412 Eye Street, N.W., Washington, D.C. 20014.

Gentlemen: Because your firm specializes in traffic cases, we should like to consult you about procedures[1] for filing with the Interstate Commerce Commission a complaint involving what we feel are discriminatory[2] rates charged by the Southern Railway for l.c.l. shipments of our unassembled furniture to several[3] states in the South.

We are also disturbed about what seem to be excessively high rates for pool-car shipments[4] to the Jones Warehouse in Portland via Union Pacific for distribution to three customers in that[5] vicinity.

May I arrange a Washington interview with a member of your firm to discuss our course of action?[6] Yours cordially, (123)

LESSON 58

278▶ To: All Rate Clerks, Subject: Filing New Tariffs.

Railroads alone may file as many as 100,000 tariffs with the Interstate Commerce Commission during[1] one year, covering changes in rates by freight, express, pipeline, and highway carriers. Keeping up to date on[2] all tariff changes so that our company products take the lowest classifications and rates available[3] is your primary responsibility. In coping with the problems that arise in getting shipments on[4] their way, however, you sometimes underestimate the value of filing new tariffs.

Please remember that nothing[5] is more important than removing from your files any rates that have been superseded and placing new ones in[6] a filing system that will give you immediate access to the latest information.

A new tariff should[7] never remain unfiled for more than one day. Nothing is more important than maintaining updated tariff files.[8] The prompt filing of new rates and the removal of superseded ones are prerequisite to getting accurate[9] tariff guidance. (182)

279▶ Waxman Packing Box Company, 700 St. Louis Road, St. Charles, Missouri 63301.

Gentlemen: Will you please ask your salesman to call with samples of wooden shooks and boxes that conform to Government[1] specifications for export shipments. Please send someone who can estimate prices to conform to special[2] needs of our irregularly shaped products for export.

In addition, we are also interested in[3] purchasing protective partitions for packaging plastic tubes, pharmaceuticals, and an assortment of electronic[4] components. We should also like to know whether any innovations have been made in your mailing tubes,[5] including No. 76, which we are now using. Sincerely yours, (110)

280▶ To: Edward R. Harmon, Director, Personnel Department, Subject: Air Credit Card No. 714.

Enclosed is an Air Credit Card to be issued, as you requested, to Herbert L. Williams, recently employed[1] in the Research and Development Laboratories. The number of the card is 18-417-031,[2] and our number is 714.

When you present Mr. Williams with his new Air Credit

Card, call his attention[3] to the instructions in the enclosed travel-arrangement guide, which he is to follow when using the services[4] of the Traffic Department. (87)

281▶ To: Harmon Jones, Purchasing Agent, Allen Shearer, International Division, Subject: New International Cargo Flight Schedules.

The new TWA Cargo Jet timetables will affect your departments. Please observe the following new schedules:[1]

Tuesdays: Flight No. 583 leaves Zurich at 7:45 p.m., arrives in New York at Kennedy[2] International Airport at 12:45 a.m. Wednesday, is transferred to Flight No. 581 and[3] leaves New York at 3:45 a.m., arriving in St. Louis at 6:44 a.m.

Thursdays: Flight No.[4] 573 leaves Geneva at 7:45 p.m., leaves Paris at 9:45 p.m., arrives[5] in New York at Kennedy International Airport at 12:45 a.m. Wednesday, is transferred to Flight[6] No. 581 and leaves New York at 3:45 a.m., arriving in St. Louis at 6:44[7] a.m.

Saturdays: Flight No. 591 leaves St. Louis at 4:35 a.m., arrives in New York at[8] 10:22 a.m., leaves New York at 12:30 p.m., arriving in Madrid at 12:25 a.m.[9] Sunday. (181)

282▶ To: Miss Lillian Heffler, Secretary to Mr. Charles C. Haynes, Director, Research and Development, Subject: Mr. Haynes's Air Reservations for New York - Boston - Washington Trip on May 26-29.

Here are the tickets for Mr. Haynes's United Airlines Flight No. 724 to New York on May 26[1] and return from Washington via TWA Flight No. 73 on May 29.

The United[2] flight offers Executive Deluxe Service, and the TWA flight offers Ambassador Red Carpet Service.[3]

Reservations were not made for the New York-Boston-Washington portions of his trip. Mr. Haynes would probably[4] prefer to use Eastern Airlines shuttle service. When he has finished his business in New York, he need only[5] go to the special check-in gate at the Eastern terminal and board the plane. The fare is collected while the plane[6] is aloft. The same type of service is available from Boston to Washington. He may use his company[7] Air-Travel Credit Card for these shuttle flights.

Traffic will be unusually heavy at the time Mr. Haynes[8] plans to go from Boston to Washington because of the Memorial Day holiday. He may prefer to have[9] a confirmed regular first-class ticket. If so, please let me know. (192)

LESSON 59

287▶ Missouri Public Service Commission, Capitol Building, Jefferson City, Missouri 65101.

Gentlemen: In the name of NATIONAL PRODUCTS, INC., Mr. Herman Briggs, attorney, and I should[1] like to request the privilege of presenting a protest against discontinuance of railway freight service[2] between Moberly, Missouri, and Ethel, Missouri, beginning June 1, 1966.

Will you please let[3] us know the date of public hearings on this petition of the Wabash Railway. Yours very truly, (78)

288▶ Freight Agent, Chicago, Burlington, and Quincy Railroad, Cedar Rapids, Iowa 52404.

Dear Sir: The First National Bank of Cedar Rapids has returned unpaid the sight draft and sight bill of lading issued[1] to Matthews Plaza Shop for our Order No. 34456 shipped on October 8.

Since the goods have[2] been in your custody beyond the allotted time for storage of shipments, we owe demurrage charges. Please include[3] them in the C. O. D. amount we must pay before the returned goods are released to us. Yours very truly,[4] (80)

289▶ Mr. Herman Briggs, Attorney, 433 Walnut Street, Moberly, Missouri 65270.

Dear Mr. Briggs: NATIONAL PRODUCTS has received permission from the Missouri Public Service Commission to[1] present a protest against the petition of the Wabash Railroad to discontinue railway freight service between[2] Moberly and Ethel on June 1. The hearings will begin in Jefferson City on March 14.

We are[3] depending on you to represent our company at that time. I plan to attend also and assist in getting[4] any additional information for your presenta-

tion as the hearings proceed.

Data about the[5] volume of shipping of our products between these points for the past three years is enclosed. I have telephoned Harry[6] Dawson, traffic manager of Phillips Cement, asking him to send similar figures about their shipments.

What[7] else can I do to help you prepare your brief? Yours truly, (150)

290▶ Mr. Monroe Wendt, Traffic Manager, Evans Manufacturing Company, 87655 St. Charles Road, Overton, Missouri 63203.

Dear Monroe: You will remember that we discussed the new Interstate Commerce Commission regulation of rates[1] for both long- and short-haul shipments on the Mississippi. Since that conversation I have talked with our Administrative[2] Committee and our legal counsel about the discriminatory features of these rates for[3] manufacturers like Miller and Evans and NATIONAL PRODUCTS.

They have authorized me to solicit the support[4] of several manufacturers in this vicinity in organizing resistance to these new rates,[5] which very clearly favor other modes of transportation.

I am, therefore, inviting you to a meeting in[6] my office on Friday, October 13, at 10 a.m., to discuss possible ways of combating these new[7] rates. Since both our United States Senators are campaigning in the state this month, I have invited them to join[8] us.

I am enclosing a list of those I suggest inviting to this meeting. I should appreciate your adding[9] or deleting any names and returning it to me so that I can issue the other invitations.[10] I am relying heavily on you, Monroe, for support in organizing and conducting this meeting. May[11] I have your ideas, please? Sincerely yours, (228)

LESSON 60

293▶ To: Branch Traffic Clerks, Subject: Changes in Shipping Instructions.

Beginning March 15, all packages weighing up to 50 pounds that were formerly sent by railway express[1] will be sent by air express.

This change will expedite deliveries. In addition, it often reduces shipping[2] costs. For instance, the cost of a 40-pound air-express package from New York to Boston is $4.70[3] versus $5.20 for railway express.

Another advantage is that air express[4] guarantees pickup within two hours after a telephone call, and delivery to customers is equally[5] fast. Armed surveillance is available for valuable packages at a reasonable rate. Air express[6] has priority after airmail on all domestic flights.

Plans for changing from railway freight to airfreight are also[7] under consideration. If any of you have had experience that would bear on a decision, please[8] tell me about it.

The decision to use air express was reached after studying comparative shipping costs[9] in the latest edition of "Leonard's Guide." To help you in making wise decisions about types of shipping to[10] choose, I am having a copy of the latest edition sent to each of you. (214)

294▶ Memo to Systems and Procedures, Subject: Your Suggestions for Revision of Routines for Making Freight Shipments.

Thank you for your promptness in returning my proposed routines for making freight shipments. I appreciate your helpful[1] suggestion in which you point out that Step C-1 duplicates Step B-5.

It is true that the inspector and[2] the packer both initial the packing slip. We have always felt that this double check contributes to the high degree[3] of accuracy in our shipping procedures and that the inspector verifies the work of the packer.[4]

We can now see that we can probably accomplish the objective of accuracy by eliminating[5] the packer's Step B-5 and leaving the accuracy check entirely to the inspector. We will follow your[6] recommendation for one month, while watching carefully to see whether the elimination of the first checkpoint[7] increases packing errors.

While we are experimenting, I recommend that we delay publishing the[8] routines. In the meantime, though, we can go ahead with the schedule you proposed for time-and-motion studies of each[9] clerk's procedures. (182)

295▶ Air and Marine Travel Service, Mayfair Hotel, 810 Locust Street, St. Louis, Missouri 63101.

Gentlemen: We are returning for reissuance a round-trip ticket via Iberian Airlines issued[1] to Miss Helen Brody of NATIONAL PRODUCTS COMPANY for a flight to Barcelona on April 17.[2]

Miss Brody has changed her plans and now wants to fly to Rome from Barcelona via TWA Flight[3] 87 on April 26 before proceeding to Zurich on Swiss Air Flight 18 on May 5. She[4] expects to return to St. Louis from Zurich as originally planned via Swiss Air to New York and via[5] TWA the rest of the way. The date of her return flight, however, has been moved up a week, to May[6] 8. The 21-day round-trip excursion fare now applies; therefore, we shall expect a refund of the difference[7] in price between the two tickets.

Please send the reissued ticket by special delivery, as Miss Brody[8] is a bit apprehensive about confirmation of her flights. Yours very truly, (175)

296▶ To: Ralph C. Akin, Sales Manager, Subject: Airplane Rental from Sales Engineer Owner.

I am inclined to approve Bill White's request to use his own plane for business trips at the commercial rate for chartered[1] planes. After all, he lives in the wide-open spaces of Texas, where commercial airplane schedules are so poor[2] that he would waste time using that method of travel. The alternative is to charter planes for his trips. He is[3] asking only that he be allowed to use his own plane at the same rate. He has a good point in saying that his[4] own plane would be safer.

My[7] only reason for not going along with this request is the precedent it sets[5] for other sales engineers. On the other hand, none of them have Bill's problems. (114)

part 3

UNITS 13-16▶ Lessons 61-80

Unit 13

LESSON 61

1 The unit in which blood transfusions or other intravenous fluids are given is 500 cubic centimeters (cm.), 500 milliliters (ml.), or 1 pint.

2 A kilogram (kg.) is equal to 1,000 grams (gm.); a milliliter (ml.) is .001 of a liter (l.); a centimeter (cm.) is .01 of a meter (m.).

3 Logic would indicate that a pill might be 30 milligrams (mg.), but it could not possibly be 30 kilograms (kg.).

4 A liter (l.) is the volume occupied by 1 kilogram (kg.) of pure water at its temperature of maximum density.

5 Thirty-two fluid ounces is equivalent to 946.333 milliliters (ml.).

6 The patient received 1 quart of blood during the operation and 500 milligrams (mg.) of aureomycin afterwards.

7 In measures of length, 3.937 inches is equal to 100 millimeters (mm.), 10 centimeters (cm.), or 1 decimeter (dm.).

8 You can convert 300 hectoliters (hl.) to liters (l.) when you divide by 100.

9 An average aspirin tablet is about 5 grains, which is approximately .3 gram (gm.) or 300 milligrams (mg.).

10 The doctor prescribed 12 tablets of medication, each 1 centigram (cg.) in weight.

297▶ Miss Catharine M. Talbott, 1240 24 Street, Lubbock, Texas 79406.

Dear Miss Talbott: Before I wrote you on May 4, I investigated two possible dates for surgery — June[1] 9 and June 27. The operating room was reserved for both dates, and tentative hospital reservations[2] were made pending your decision.

I have just found out, however, that an emergency will take me out[3] of Houston on June 26 and keep me away until July 3. It will be necessary, therefore, to[4] withdraw the June 27 date. I have again checked the schedule and find that there is still a surgery date[5] open on June 11 as well as on June 9.

I hope that you can arrange for the operation on either[6] the 9th or the 11th. If you can do this, I can be here long enough after your surgery to be[7] sure that you are progressing satisfactorily before I leave.

Please telephone me promptly to tell me the[8] date you wish to reserve, as all tentative arrangements must be confirmed two weeks before the patient expects to[9] enter the hospital for surgery. Please tell me also whether you wish to reserve a semiprivate or[10] a private room.

You are expected to check into the hospital by two o'clock the afternoon before your[11] operation. The enclosed instruction sheet provides further information about your preparation for the[12] operation. Sincerely yours, (243)

298▶ Dr. Warren C. Smith, Medical Plaza, Amarillo, Texas 79103.

Dear Doctor Smith: Patient: Mary Lee Long, File No. 3134. The above patient was examined in the[1] medical clinic on January 18. Because she is moving to Amarillo on February 5,[2] she has asked me to send you a report of our findings.

At the time of the examination, she complained[3] of pain in her right knee. There were no other symptoms. The pain began about six months ago and has been intermittent[4] since that time. She now feels that the periods of discomfort are becoming of longer duration and[5] greater frequency. Examination showed the right knee to be limited in flexion because of pain, but the[6] left knee was normal.

Mrs. Long was referred to the Wilson Clinic, where it was thought that her pain was due to[7] spasm on the right side, probably because of an injury to the right foot sustained several months ago in[8] a fall. A series of exercises was prescribed for her. Pads for her shoes were prescribed, but she refused to wear[9] them.

She is coming in during her last week in Houston for X rays; and if we find any pathological[10] symptoms, we will notify you. Thank you for referring Mrs. Long to us. Sincerely yours, (217)

* * *

▶ If your boss makes frequent changes in his dictation, you can eliminate confusion by taking notes in only one column of each notebook page. A correction can be made directly across from the material that has been changed.

299▶ Dr. Alvin R. Christian, 411 Main Street, Big Spring, Texas 79722.

Dear Doctor Christian: Your patient, Mrs. Amy Green, was discharged from the hospital today. We have asked her to[1] see you for postoperative treatment; but if you would like us to see her at any time, we shall be most happy[2] to do so.

Our examination resulted in the same diagnosis you had made — hernia of the sinus.[3] This was repaired without difficulty. She was kept in the hospital for close observation for three days[4] after the operation, and she made a very satisfactory recovery. Her temperature was[5] never above normal except for the brief period when she was recovering from the anaesthesia.[6]

There is no reason to expect recurrence of the hernia or any complications during her recovery.[7] Sincerely yours, (143)

300▶ Lone Star Insurance Company, 141 South Sixth Street, Fort Worth, Texas 76117.

Gentlemen: This letter answers your inquiry about Mrs. J. S. Adams.

Mrs. Adams has never been[1] hospitalized at our institution. She was examined in our Outpatient Department two years ago, when[2] a cinder was removed from the left eye. A second visit indicated that any damage to the eye was[3] superficial.

These two visits represent the

only times when she was treated or examined at this hospital.[4]

I hope that this information will be helpful to you in disposing of her claim. Yours very truly,[5] (100)

301▸ Mrs. Wilma A. Whiter, 432 Jackson Street, Dallas, Texas 77414.

Dear Mrs. Whiter: We have made an appointment for you at the hospital for a basal metabolism[1] test on Tuesday morning, March 21, at nine o'clock.

The purpose of this test is to measure the amount of[2] oxygen you consume under relaxed conditions. To get the best results, I suggest that you spend the night in[3] Houston rather than travel from Dallas the morning of the test. Please follow these further instructions:

1. Eat a[4] light supper the evening before the test.

2. Go to bed no later than ten o'clock the night before the test.[5]

3. Do not rush when you get up in the morning; omit any exercises; dress slowly.

4. Do not eat breakfast.[6] This means that you are to have nothing to eat or drink, except water, after supper the night before.

5. Do[7] not smoke the morning of the test.

6. Do not walk to the hospital; go to the hospital with as little[8] exercise as possible. Sincerely yours, (170)

302▸ Mr. Wesley J. Higgins, 1419 Oak Lane, Galveston, Texas 77551.

Dear Mr. Higgins: I sent your completed application for reimbursement for medical services and[1] hospitalization to the Hospital Plan headquarters. Although you asked that the completed form be returned[2] to you, I could not comply with your request, as it violates the regulations of the insurance company.[3]

Very strict rules govern the procedures for obtaining reimbursement for charges that have already been[4] paid. I am sure that you realize that we want to help you to conform to these regulations so that you will[5] be repaid as soon as possible. Ordinarily the hospital and physician are paid by the insurance[6] plan; therefore, this case is extraordinary. Sincerely yours, (132)

303▸ Mr. Henry E. Barnett, District Director, Federal Bureau of Investigation, Room 322, Federal Building, Dallas, Texas 75200.

Dear Mr. Barnett: Subject: William Robertson Autopsy. My report on the Robertson autopsy, along[1] with the X rays, is enclosed.

In my opinion, the hemorrhage was caused by trauma. It is not necessary[2] to have a skull fracture in order to have cranial hemorrhage; I have seen it caused on several occasions[3] by a blow or by bumping the head against something hard.

Should you have any questions about the autopsy[4] findings, I shall be glad to attempt to answer them for you. Sincerely yours, (94)

304▶ Miss Emily Weber, Oakdale Convalescent Home, 766 Oakdale Terrace, Norman, Oklahoma 73069.

Dear Miss Weber: When you checked out of the hospital, you gave us the number of your Blue Shield contract, which covers[1] your medical bills, rather than the number of your Blue Cross contract, which covers hospitalization.

We must[2] have the correct Blue Cross number so that we can prepare the papers necessary for our reimbursement for[3] your recent stay in Metropolitan Hospital. Our claim must be filed within five days after your release; so[4] please send the information at once, using the enclosed envelope, which is marked for my attention. Yours very[5] cordially, (101)

LESSON 63

305▶ Dr. Harold C. Shelley, First National Bank Building, Dallas, Texas 75201.

Dear Doctor Shelley: Joseph West, File 19887. The following report is based on my tests of, and[1] interviews with, this 29-year-old male, whom you referred for a consultant's opinion.

The hospital diagnosis[2] is neuritis, intercostal; epilepsy, grand mal. The patient has had two typical grand mal seizures[3] since his admission to the hospital; but his current complaints seem to involve mainly a severe pain in[4] the head, occasional inability to focus his eyes, and increased irritability and confusion[5] in thinking.

On the Rorschach test the patient gave a rather unusual, mixed record of 32[6] responses. At the time of this test the patient stated that his eyes would not focus, and he went through the entire test[7] having one eye covered with his hand. The record seems to reflect a rather varied personality picture.[8] There are elements that are similar to what has been called "a typical epileptic record," marked by a[9] poorly controlled use of color. Other aspects point to the presence of a marked neurotic tendency. Anxiety[10] and depression are shown rather clearly, with additional suggestions of negativism and[11] opposition to external influences. Basic personality strength is adequate, but he suffers from[12] lack of mature integration and stability. There is no evidence of current or impending loss of[13] contact with reality, although there is a moderate degree of neurotic confusion.

Eleven cards[14] of an apperception test were administered in an attempt to understand better the dynamic development[15] of this personality structure. In general, the stories were somewhat poorly developed and[16] integrated and may tend to corroborate an earlier impression of immaturity in the patient's[17] approach to problems. There are more or less specific hints of early parental rejection with accompanying[18] hostility . and guilt feelings, especially toward the father. Almost all the stories were given happy[19] endings, again suggesting a lack of mature realism in the patient's thinking.

This patient appears to[20] be operating currently at a high-average intellectual level, although there is probably[21] a significant loss of efficiency in his present functioning. The Rorschach test protocol shows some[22] similarity to what has been called an "epileptic record." More reliable signs, however, tend to indicate[23] a neurotic element in the personality picture, with anxiety components predominating.[24] The basic personality strength seems to be quite adequate and, although it is poorly integrated[25] at this time, suggests little possibility of an impending psychosis. Yours very truly,[26] (520)

306▶ INCIDENCE OF SURGERY IN DIABETES.

The modern treatment of diabetes, which began with the discovery and use of insulin, has nearly[1] eliminated diabetes itself by means of surgery. Other factors have improved the care of[2] elderly diabetics, including more deliberate preparation for surgery, intravenous feeding,[3] and, most of all, the use of sulfonamides and the antibiotics. Operative surgery and modern[4] diabetic treatment have so prolonged the lives of patients with the dreaded infections and gangrenous lesions[5] of the feet that the duration of life after recovery from such operations has

made the total[6] duration of life after onset of diabetes almost equal to the average for all persons of that[7] age.

Diabetic surgery foreshadows the preventive surgery of the future. An infection makes a[8] diabetic worse, but surgical procedure can remove infected teeth, tonsils, appendix, gallbladder, or[9] kidney, and bring to an end infections of the feet. Although an increased metabolism transforms a mild[10] diabetic into a severe one, the surgeon can relieve the hyperthyroidism by removal of thyroid[11] and transform the diabetic back to his original and usually benign state. Much is heard of[12] preventive medicine; more should be heard of preventive surgery. (253)

LESSON 64

308▶ Dr. Joseph Foley, Department of Neurology, Boston City Hospital, Boston, Massachusetts 02116.

Dear Joe: A fascinating patient of mine was a summer visitor here from South Boston. I should like you to[1] follow up on this case, as she is returning home next week.

This 11-year-old girl had a head injury[2] that appeared to be insignificant. While running down a pathway, she fell and struck her head on a stone. She was[3] not knocked unconscious, and she went into the house. Within 5 or 10 minutes of the fall, she began to notice[4] some numbness of her left arm; within 15 minutes she was drowsy; and within 45 minutes she was in[5] coma. She was rushed up here, and in an hour and a half skull films were taken. She was in a wild and restless coma,[6] with bilateral Babinskis; the skull films were negative. Despite this, I suspected she might have a meningeal[7] hemorrhage and did bilateral temporal burr holes, which were negative.

Postoperatively, on[8] the first and second day she remained in coma and began developing focal seizures in the left side of[9] her face and in her left arm and hand. These were extremely difficult to control with medication, and she really[10] went into a focal status that confused me greatly. I finally decided to look again at[11] the operative temporal incisions, wondering whether she could have bled from the side of the burr holes. Since[12] they were so negative the first time, I could not believe any pathology then would lead to the focal seizures.[13] At 48 hours, however, reopening of the burr holes was completely negative once again, and[14] her focal status continued.

Therefore, on the fourth postoperative day, because of the development of[15] some stiffness of the neck, a rising blood pressure, and a slowing pulse, I put in some cerebellar burr holes over[16] the occipital bone in keeping with our extreme interest in trauma to the posterior fossa,[17] which we are in the process of writing up. Here, to my gratification, we found a subdural hygroma,[18] which was under pressure. From this time

on the child began to improve and stopped convulsing within 48 hours,[19] her state of consciousness steadily improved, and she is now about ready for discharge. She is up and about[20] and is seizure-free. She is going home approximately next Tuesday, August 13, with rather an extraordinary[21] recovery.

She is going to be sent to the Rehabilitation Center for therapy[22] directed at reeducation of her left arm and left leg, which are not spastic at all and are improving[23] greatly. When she will be able to return to school, I am not exactly sure; I will leave that to your judgment.[24]

I appreciate very much your seeing her and should also like to know how she gets along. Very truly[25] yours, (501)

* * *

▸ Date your shorthand notebook at the bottom of each page. This procedure will save you time when trying to locate old notes.

LESSON 65

311▸ CLINICAL RECORD PSYCHOLOGICAL DATA

The patient, a 29-year-old white male, was referred for psychologic evaluation.

The patient complained[1] of poor appetite and continued low back pains, from which various other pains radiated. He manifested[2] a great deal of overt hostility, saying, "I will get adequate medical care if it has to[3] be at the point of a pistol." He expressed vehemently his dislike of the medical care he has received[4] and further verbalized feelings of distrust of everyone. The patient admits entertaining suicidal[5] thoughts. At the end of the first interview, he stated that he was willing to bear with the continuation[6] of testing, saying, "If you want to do this so that you can put me in jail, it's O.K. with me." Throughout the[7] testing sessions, his behavior seemed disorganized.

The Minnesota Multiphasic Personality[8] Inventory was administered with questionable results. The picture presented must be interpreted with[9] caution, since one of the validating scores falls close to the upper limits of the normal range. With the exception[10] of the masculinity-femininity score, the whole profile falls above the upper limits of this[11] normal range. Since this is the case, it is difficult to say more than that the patient is markedly disturbed and[12] to note that the highest scores were obtained on the schizophrenia and depression scales. It is of interest[13] that paranoia is not one of the highest scores.

The Rorschach test was limited to thirteen responses, with[14] rejections on the seventh and ninth cards. Although at present he appears to be somewhat outgoing, there seems to[15] be a trend toward withdrawal from interpersonal contacts. There is some suggestion of unrealistic thinking[16] in his verbalizations.

The patient is of average intelligence. The testing picture suggests a[17] markedly disturbed individual who seems to be losing control and is possibly at a prepsychotic[18] level of development. Little can be inferred from the record as to the source of his difficulty. At[19] this point the patient seems to fluctuate between periods of adequate and inadequate organization[20] of his thought processes. Chief Clinical Psychologist (410)

* * *

▶ A gentle but thorough eraser and an erasure shield are essential if you want your transcribed material to look its best. If satisfactory erasers and erasure shields cannot be obtained through your office, buy your own. Necessary corrections will be made quickly and efficiently, and your typed work will be free of unsightly smudges.

Unit 14————————————

Secretarial Assignment

1 According to the NEC (National Electrical Code), all electric outlets must be properly protected.

2 Please exchange the 30 w (watt) bulb for a 100 w (watt) bulb.

3 What commonly used element has an at wt (atomic weight) of 55.85 and a sp gr (specific gravity) of 7.86 at 20 C (degrees Centigrade)?

4 Can you play both $33\frac{1}{3}$ rpm (revolutions per minute) and 45 rpm (revolutions per minute) records on your player?

5 The flow of the system is less than the rated 5 gpm (gallons per minute).

6 One kw (kilowatt) of electricity equals 1,000 w (watts).

7 Add 8 kg per cu m (kilograms per cubic meter) of Ethynol to the experimental batch.

8 The additives changed the reaction by .005 fnp (fusion point).

9 The new tests showed a satisfactory improvement of emf (electromotive force).

10 The fp (freezing point) of water is reached at 32 F (degrees Fahrenheit); but on other thermometer scales the fp (freezing point) is zero.

LESSON 66

312▶ ASPECTS OF SCIENCE

Science is already valued for what it can do to increase man's control over nature, and feared for what some[1] of its consequences may be. Science aims at understanding the nature of things; in this it is at one with[2] religion and philosophy. But its approach is the opposite. Science begins by studying details, often[3] trivial details, which are queer and appeal to human curiosity — things like black rocks, which attract iron,[4] or rubbed amber, which makes chaff fly.

From the study of details come concepts. Concepts are the bases for hypotheses[5] and laws. They are the things that get names such as mass, energy, temperature, entropy, wavelength, charge,[6] electrons, and quantum numbers.

Some do not survive, such as caloric and phlogiston. Others are deposed from their[7] independence and become vassals of the more successful, as mass has become a vassal of energy or[8] valency of electronic structure.

But the successful concepts are not concerned with details any more. They[9] penetrate deep into the heart of things. Electrons, for example, are regarded as present in all ordinary[10] matter; and in any attempt to explain the behavior of matter — physical, chemical, or[11] ultimately biological—one is forced back onto them. At present they stand as a fundamental concept;[12] but even when they ultimately come under some still more general idea, the concept of an electron[13] will still be used, as mass is in mechanics.

Scientific concepts enable certain aspects of the[14] enormous complexity of the world to be handled by men's minds. They are suggested mostly by experiment[15] but partly by mathematics, and they are controlled by the need that they should not lead to illogical consequences.[16] (320)

313▶ MASS, ENERGY, AND MATTER

Mass is only one property of matter, and perhaps not even the most important. There are indications[1] that matter is not just another name for energy. The study of the many curious particles that[2] have been found in cosmic rays and in water produced in giant atomsmashers has shown the persistence of certain[3] features in spite of the bewildering number of spontaneous changes that these particles undergo.[4] Two groups of these particles have appeared such that the net number in each group remains always the same, and this in[5] contrast to a third group for which there is no constancy. Net number refers to the difference between the numbers[6] of the ordinary particles and the antiparticles. Thus electrons are a member of one group[7] called leptons, to which neutrinos also belong. In reckoning the net number of electrons, one subtracts the[8] number of positrons from the number of ordinary electrons. Thus the creation of an electron-positron[9] pair does not alter the net number. The rule states that no interaction between particles of any[10] kind, including the photons of radiant energy and the mesons of the cosmic rays, can alter the[11] sum of the net numbers of the three kinds of particles — electrons, neutrinos, and mesons — which count as leptons.[12] A similar rule holds for the class of particles — protons, neutrons, and some others, which rank as baryons. Leptons[13] can never change into baryons, or reversely.

This seems to hint that underlying matter are two classes[14] of entity, each of which can indeed appear in several different forms, with various amounts of[15] mass, sometimes electrically charged and sometimes not, but yet fundamentally the same. Matter is more than merely[16] mass or energy. A neutrino has zero rest mass, but yet it is an entity. A piece of ordinary[17] matter is made up of leptons and baryons in fixed numbers. (351)

* * *

▸ Avoid eyestrain by placing your notebook in an upright position when you transcribe. Some notebooks have specially treated edges that enable them to stand in an upright position without additional support. Otherwise, a copyholder can be used to support the notebook in an upright position.

LESSON 67

314▸ BIOLOGY AND ENGINEERING

Knowledge of the fundamental workings of the life process can have far-reaching implications and values. The[1] improvements to be achieved in human performance and tolerance to stress are closely related to medical[2] interest in control of disease and are well known. But less well known is the potential application of[3] biology in engineering. Physical scientists are making slow progress in building complex computer[4] devices that can imitate the element of judgment characteristic of animal or human[5] behavior. So far, machines can do what they are programmed to do, but they can do little learning. Engineers now[6] look with renewed interest on the ways nature has solved her control and communication problems. Nature has[7] served as a vast laboratory for over two billion years and has made uncountable experiments. This[8] vast evolutionary process has resulted in a fantastic wealth of animal types, many with unique[9] and highly developed characteristics far beyond those of man. It is important that engineers look[10] at all kinds of special senses in animals, and at the kinds of nervous control exhibited by even[11] the simpler forms of life. The comparative approach to the solutions of biological problems has been[12] a profitable strategy in the past and will undoubtedly be expanded as biology becomes[13] a more quantitative and analytical science.

A better understanding of man's behavior is recognized[14] to be critical for the broad areas of selection, training, and efficiency. Since behavior[15] depends upon differentiation within the central nervous system, the correlation of behavior[16] with nervous activity should be as broad as possible and should not overlook the highly developed and[17] stereotyped behaviors of certain species that may exemplify a relatively simple correlation[18] between nervous structure and function. It should be far simpler to analyze the nervous system of an[19] insect with a few nervous components than to tackle the intricate and frightening networks that comprise the[20] nervous system of a rat or a monkey or a man.

Today missiles are all the rage. The missile is a stupid[21] beast, however, since it goes only where you tell it to go. Unless you know where to send it, it is virtually[22] worthless. A manned airplane is infinitely more versatile than a missile.

But a missile operated[23] by a computer that works like a man's brain would make the manned plane obsolete. This is what is being sought in[24] the biology basic-research program. (487)

315▸ TRANSISTORS

The features responsible for the rapid and widespread acceptance of the transistor are reliability,[1] ruggedness, small size and weight, and independence from the hot, and therefore power-consuming, source of[2] electrons required by the vacuum tube. Inherently, the transistor is a simpler device to manufacture[3] than the vacuum tube.

As with diodes and rectifiers, transistors are made either from germanium or[4] silicon. Basically, all transistors consist of three active elements: the emitter, which is analogous[5] to the cathode of the vacuum tube; the collector, which is equivalent to the tube's plate; and the base,[6] which serves as the grid and lies between the emitter and the collector. Very small electrical signals applied[7] to the base act as a valve in controlling the flow of current between the emitter and the collector.[8] When connected to appropriate electrical circuitry, the transistor can amplify weak signals,[9] oscillate and generate high frequency signals of its own, and act as an electric switch. Therefore, the[10] transistor can replace the vacuum tube if the requirements of temperature, frequency, and power-handling capabilities[11] lie within its operating range.

The transistor has, in fact, replaced the vacuum tube in hearing[12] aids and portable radios; in many types of electrical instruments, computers, industrial control[13] equipment; and in a large array of military control, guidance, and communications equipment.[14] Many vast, new applications depend on extension of the operating characteristics and on cost[15] reduction. Such applications include fully transistorized car radios and portable television[16] sets, vehicle fuel injection and ignition systems to provide greater fuel economy, and automotive[17] voltage regulators to permit battery charging at idling speeds. (355)

316▶ Memo to Arthur Williamson, Manager of Public Information, Subject: Cobalt-60 Release.

As you requested on January 9, we have asked our technical writers to submit the following[1] material about our plans for increased production of Cobalt-60 for release on January 17.[2] I hope you won't think that the material is too technical for publication in a business magazine;[3] but if you do, give me a call so that we can attempt to simplify it further.

The Universal[4] Electric Company, the only commercial producer of Cobalt-60 in the United States, is taking[5] preliminary steps to double the production of the radioactive material next year. Company[6] scientists in Baltimore are already in the process of increasing power in their test reactor[7] to its present permissible operating maximum — 50 megawatts. (154)

LESSON 68

317▶ BINARY DIGIT

Recently the notion of ultimate units has been applied to the communications field and has opened[1] the way to important advances in the design of calculating machines and to a better understanding[2] of the working of the brain. The art of communication is very old, but the science is very new.[3] When speed was reduced to syllables and an alphabet was built, the first great steps in the right direction were taken,[4] for letters are comparable to the atoms of chemistry. All communication is a matter of[5] information conveyed by signals, and the next great step was atomic signals. The bulk of signals were and are[6] analogical. They are signals in which a value of some continuously varying quantity stands[7] for the message, like the current in your telephone or the distance on your slide rule. The difficulty with such[8] signals is that their precision is limited to about six significant figures at best. Hence, the information[9] that analogical signals can convey is inadequate for many of the requirements of modern[10] science.

There is another kind of signal in which some variable is restricted to a small number[11] of possible values at distinct times or separate places. This is the famous binary digit, now[12] nicknamed "bit." Any number can be written in bits as well as in the decimal system. In the binary[13] system, 1, 2, 3, 4, and 5 become simply 1, 10, 11, 100, and 101.

The use[14] of the binary digits 0 and 1 conforms to what is perhaps the simplest part of logic. The logic[15] of relations is reduced to the logic of classes when only one relation is considered, such as[16] membership in some class. The logic of classes is reduced to the logic of propositions when membership in only[17] one class is considered, such as the class of truths. The value 1 is then assigned to anything if it is[18] true; if not, 0 is assigned. In fact, the discovery of this property led to the attempts to construct[19] a logical machine. Today any device for communication that performs its computations by discrete[20] signals is referred to as either a "digital" or a "logical" machine.

The scope of any communication[21] device is ultimately determined by the number of distinct states that it enjoys. Since the world[22] is composed of particles that can only be in discrete states, all machines can be tested as if they were digital[23] devices if full use can be made of all these particles in their states.

It is not yet possible to[24] weigh one electron more or less or to measure the position of a pointer to the least possible jump of[25] nuclear dimensions. These can be dealt with statisti-

cally; and when this is done, the theoretically[26] distinguishable states of the system on the average are ignored. (533)

318▶ THE SIGNAL IN THE TELEVISION SET

In the simplest television system, in which radio waves are not used, the essential components are the[1] camera and synchronization generator, which produce the picture signal, including the blanking and[2] synchronizing pulses. The picture signal travels along a cable to the receiver. In the course of the[3] journey, the orderly electron motions of the signal current gradually weaken as the electrons[4] collide with the metal ions of the cable wires. If the cable is longer than a mile or two, there must be[5] amplifiers to offset the weakening process and keep the strength of the signal above the level of the[6] noise currents. Under these conditions the signal will reach the end of a cable in a reasonable state of[7] preservation, uncontaminated by noticeable noise and free of smear and overshoot.

At the receiving[8] end of the cable, the picture signal is separated into the two parts that carry respectively[9] the synchronizing and picture information. These two types of information occur on either side of the[10] blanking level of the wave, the sync information below and the picture information above. By passing[11] the signal through a sync separation amplifier that responds only to the parts of the signal below[12] the blanking level, the sync information is separated from the picture information. The separated[13] sync pulses are then used to control the deflection generators, which pass the deflecting currents through the[14] coils around the neck of the picture tube. The position of the electron beam is thereby forced to move across[15] the screen in strict step with the beam in the camera.

The picture signal is applied to the electron gun, and[16] it controls the current in the electron beam, so that the light produced on the screen varies from point to point along[17] each scanning line. The picture signal is first amplified to increase its overall voltage to about 60[18] volts. When so magnified, the picture voltage is capable of turning the beam from full on to full off; that[19] is, from maximum screen brightness to darkness.

When the electron beam is thus controlled as to direction by[20] correctly timed deflection currents and as to current by the picture signal, the picture tube produces on its[21] screen the desired picture pattern of lights and shadows. (430)

LESSON 69

320▶ LIMITATIONS OF SPACE FLIGHT

When the first American satellite went into orbit, there were instruments aboard that gave an indication[1] of a very high radiation field outside the earth's atmosphere. This finding was definitely confirmed[2] when the next satellite was placed in orbit. It was soon found that the radiations involved were quite different[3] from the cosmic rays, and it appeared that the intensities were great enough to be a real hazard for manned[4] space vehicles.

It has been found that the radiations consist almost entirely of electrons and protons[5] and are confined largely to two zones surrounding the earth, with maximum concentrations occurring in the plane[6] of the magnetic equator. The peak intensity in each zone occurs roughly at 3,500 and[7] 18,000 kilometers from the surface of the earth. They are usually referred to as the Van Allen[8] radiation belts, after their discoverer.

Present theories of these radiation belts postulate[9] that the particles are trapped by the earth's magnetic field and may remain there for a considerable period[10] of time. As an electron or proton travels toward the earth from the sun, it encounters the earth's magnetic[11] field, which deflects the particle toward either the north or south polar regions in such a way that it spirals around[12] a line of force. As the particle approaches the earth, the converging magnetic lines of force cause it to[13] be reflected along the same line toward the opposite pole, where the process is repeated. Thus, the particle[14] may continue its back-and-forth motion for days or perhaps months.

Although the origin of charged particles in[15] the radiation belts has not been fully established, it appears that most, if not all, are of solar origin.[16] One hypothesis assumes that the particles of the two belts have different origins. According to this[17] hypothesis, those of the outer belt originate in the sun, perhaps as a result of a solar eruption,[18] and after being trapped in the geomagnetic field are lost slowly by collision with the very sparse[19] atmosphere. They are then replenished at the next time of solar activity. In times of violent solar[20] activity, the particles spill over in large numbers in the upper atmosphere in the polar regions,[21] thus accounting for the aurorae. (425)

LESSON 70

322▶ 3M'S QUICK PROCESS DEVELOPS COLOR PRINTS THAT WON'T FADE, CURL, OR YELLOW WITH AGE

Minnesota Mining & Manufacturing Company has a machine that will produce full-color prints from[1] color negatives in less than five minutes.

Aiming at the industrial, military, and graphic arts market,[2] 3M has developed a print process in which color dyes are electroplated on zinc oxide paper.[3] Called "Electrocolor," the technique does not require the silver halides or stop baths used in conventional[4] processes and involves only one adjustment by the operator: he focuses the negative and determines[5] how long the paper must be exposed. Once the negative image is focused on the paper, the rest of

the[6] operation is automatic.

Inside the machine, the paper is exposed to blue light, then dipped in a yellow[7] dye, electroplated, washed with hot water, and dried; the process is repeated with green and red light, magenta[8] and cyan dyes. According to 3M, the finished product may cost slightly more than prints processed by conventional[9] techniques; but when protected with a polymer coating, it won't fade, curl, or yellow with age. 3M will[10] lease the machine to customers. (206)

323▶ LIMITATIONS OF SCIENTIFIC CERTAINTY

Something needs to be said about the inner nature of science and technology and of scientists and[1] engineers. Certain things must be understood by all the world if we are to operate practically in the[2] condition of moral unneutrality that has been invoked. These inner qualities really turn out to be[3] special limits on science and technology. To state it baldly, scientifically there are limits on[4] truth, there are limits on certainty, and there are limits on discovery itself. Maybe the limit on certainty[5] is the most important. Scientific findings and scientific facts are usually thought of as[6] symbols of certainty. But people must realize that these findings are certain only with respect to a[7] particular frame of reference. That frame of reference is the present state of knowledge or the present position[8] of scientific thought. Of paramount importance is the knowledge that in order to progress it is[9] necessary to recognize the ignorance and leave room for doubt. Scientific knowledge is a body of statements[10] of varying degrees of certainty—some most unsure, some nearly sure, none absolutely certain. Scientists[11] are used to this and take it for granted that it is perfectly consistent to be unsure—that it is[12] possible to live and not know. And so the world, facing the possibility of an era blessed by the fruits of[13] science, must learn to accept the uncertainties of science.

Correspondingly, the truth is also subject to[14] drastic revision in the light of discovery. Note carefully the difference between this kind of revision[15] of truth and that in which the truth is compared to falsehood, deceit, or clumsy human error. Indeed, since wave[16] mechanics has supplemented classical mechanics in the description of material events, the[17] scientists' own concepts of truth and certainty have dramatically changed. But much of the popular view of science[18] is still related to the deterministic description of the state of a physical system. Technically,[19] this reached its climax in the revelation of the basis of laws governing the motion of the[20] heavenly bodies. However, in atomic physics this casual deterministic account has been vigorously[21] displaced by the quantum theory, involving a universal quantum of action. Thus, for nearly sixty[22] years the physicist, and later the chemist, have had to make experimental conditions such that they could[23] describe universally their findings without being dependent upon a particular quantum that was[24] being observed at that particular time. In other words, to make these experiments anything like a truthful[25] description, it has been necessary to work with such heavy-handed measurements that the individual[26] quanta of action were completely disregarded.

The scientists of our age and also the engineers[27] who work with nuclear physics and with the tools of solid-state electronics, like transistors and magnets, have[28] already come to terms with the kind of uncertainty and incomplete truth with which they must live. But, along with[29] this, of course, there is a quantization of truth. Never can the scientist deal with a half truth. The scientist[30] has to tell the whole truth as he knows it in that movement in time, and nothing less or different can be expected.[31] (620)

Unit 15

324▶ Mr. Clyde N. Smith, 2274 Ohio Avenue, Richmond, Indiana 47374.

Dear Mr. Smith: Mr. and Mrs. James Nye, holders of the mortgage on your residence property, have placed the[1] notes and mortgages in our hands for foreclosure.

You no doubt realize that

foreclosure proceedings will cause the[2] whole amount of the mortgage to become due and payable and may impose on you the further obligations[3] of paying attorneys' fees and costs of foreclosure. The records turned over to us indicate that you have omitted[4] payment on the last five monthly installments and are delinquent, therefore, in the amount of[5] $2,350.

We have been instructed to institute proceedings for foreclosure at once, but it[6] is our feeling that you should have one more opportunity to clear these delinquent payments. If satisfactory[7] arrangements for payment of these overdue amounts have not been made before the first of next month, we shall start[8] foreclosure proceedings without further notice to you. Yours very truly, (170)

325▶ Dr. Harry L. Wilson, 1272 Medical Arts Building, South Meridan Street, Indianapolis, Indiana 46201.

Dear Doctor Wilson: Re: John Smith and Jane Smith v. Peter Jones. John Smith and his wife Jane are in my office as[1] I dictate this letter. I believe that they have informed you that we are handling their damage suit against Peter[2] Jones.

I have made a vigorous effort to settle this case out of court, but I have received no cooperation[3] from the adjuster for the insurance company. I feel that it is now my duty to file a suit.

Please[4] send me a résumé, in nontechnical language, of the injuries sustained by both Mr.

and Mrs. Smith[5] so that I may properly cover the subject in the preparation of the complaint.

It is further requested[6] that you send your entire bill as well as an estimate of the amount you may need to charge in the future[7] to conclude treatment. Yours very truly, (146)

326▶ Mr. William H. Hamilton, 346 Oak Street, Gary, Indiana 46402.

Dear Mr. Hamilton: State of Indiana v. Edgar Shaw and Sons (Herbert and Walter). I have checked the[1] law in regard to the question of your right to sue for default of their official bonds by the defendants in the[2] above case. We have reached the conclusion that you can maintain this action.

Therefore, have the records of the City[3] Clerk in Gary checked for the details of the bonds. The enclosed form will aid you in recording the pertinent[4] data required for preparing the complaint. Be sure to include the names of the officers of the Citizens[5] Bonding Company, Inc., which signed the bonds.

As soon as you obtain this information, bring it to[6] this office and sign a verification to the complaint. We will then proceed to file suit in the matter. Sincerely yours, (141)

327▶ Hill Brothers, 235 Locust Street, Cameron, Missouri 64429.

Gentlemen: Re: Albert Simms. Based on the information contained in your letter about the sale of groceries[1] to Albert Simms, a minor, it is our positive opinion that you can collect, in court if necessary,[2] for these goods. The law definitely states that a minor is obligated on his contract for necessities.[3] Mr. Simms could not use minority as a defense against payment of your bill unless it could be proved that[4] he bought luxury foods not commonly consumed by persons "in his station in life."

Another reason you have[5] a case is that any minor is emancipated by marriage and becomes responsible for all debts[6] contracted by him after his marriage. For your further information, it is an established principle of law[7] that a minor's contract that is recognized and endorsed by him after he has reached legal age is thereby[8] validated by him and binding upon him. The fact that Mr. Simms wrote to you after he attained his majority[9] to protest the amount of the bill gives you additional protection. Yours very truly, (198)

* * *

▶ If you use a fountain pen during dictation, be sure that it has an ample ink supply. Fill your pen each morning and after each long dictation session. Always be sure to have a few pencils at hand during dictation in case your pen runs out of ink.

LESSON 72

328▶ Mr. Morris T. Fellows, 142 Exchange Building, Richmond, Virginia 23216.

Dear Mr. Fellows: In re: J. B.

Crane. We have talked with Mr. Crane and cannot obtain payment. In the first place,[1] he disputes the bill, stating that he has received statements showing the balance due to be $275[2] instead of $375. He does not seem to have satisfactory evidence[3] to substantiate this contention. However, after investigating his financial condition, we[4] feel sure that we could not collect $375 even if we had a judgment.

We will follow[5] up the case and will let you hear from us if there are any further developments. Sincerely yours, (119)

329▶ Mr. James W. Langston, Johnson Sales Agency, 378 Barker Building, Cincinnati, Ohio 45225.

Dear Mr. Langston: Your letter of February 9, in which you inquire about the balance outstanding[1] on the account of Charles C. Matthews, was referred to me for appropriate action. The debtor failed to settle[2] the account in full; consequently, we have taken a transcript from the Justice of the Peace and filed it with the[3] Clerk of Courts in Cincinnati, Ohio.

You also inquired about Mr. Young. He has been notified that[4] unless he makes a settlement in full on or before Monday, March 10, we will bring a creditor's bill to sell[5] his real estate. We cannot believe that he will allow the matter to drag on and thus incur the expense[6] of a suit in the Common Pleas Court. Sincerely yours, (130)

330▶ Messrs, Nutley & Crom-

well, 118 Front Street, Talla-
hassee, Florida 32301.

Gentlemen: Your claim has
been turned over to this department from our Complaint Department. After investigating,[1]
we find that the box sent us ar-
rived in good condition and
showed no signs of rough handling. However, when the[2]
goods were unpacked, they
proved to be so badly scratched
that we refused to accept the
merchandise.

The claim agent of[3] the Boston & Albany Railroad, after in-
specting the shipment, was positive that the damage must have
occurred[4] before the shipment
was accepted by the railroad
company; and he took the box
away with him. While we[5] want
to be perfectly fair in the matter,
we do not see just how you can
hold us responsible for goods
that[6] we refused to accept. As
Mr. Anderson, of our Complaint
Department, has written you, if
you will duplicate[7] the order
with perfect goods, we will accept them and will mail you a
check as soon as we are billed.
Sincerely[8] yours, (161)

**331▶ The James K. Little Com-
pany, 267 North Broad Street,
Philadelphia, Pennsylvania
19101.**

Gentlemen: In re: Charles T.
Allen. In order to obtain payment on the two notes issued to
you by Mr.[1] Charles T. Allen,
our attorney entered suit, obtained judgment, issued execu-
tion, and levied on some[2] furniture, which was subsequently
sold by the sheriff. We suc-

ceeded in collecting $203.30,[3]
two-thirds of the original debt,
less the credit memorandum of
$9.25, which[4] as payee's agent
we endorsed on one of the notes.

We are therefore enclosing
our check for $194.05.[5] Sincere-
ly yours, (106)

332▶ CONTRACT

This Contract, made and con-
cluded this first day of April,
1966, by and between Hilder-
man-Smith[1] Electronics, of 300
South Gate Street, Phoenix, Arizona, party of the first part, and
Harold K. Harrison,[2] of 5400
Eagle Drive, Seattle, Washington, party of the second part.

The said party of the second[3]
part covenants and agrees to
and with the party of the first
part, to furnish his services to
the said[4] party of the first part
as special demonstrator and
representative for the period of
six months, beginning[5] May 1,
1966, and expiring October 31,
1966; and the said party[6] of the
second part convenants and
agrees to perform faithfully all
duties incident to such employment.[7]

The said party of the first part
covenants and agrees to pay
the said party of the second
part, for the[8] same, the sum of
$3,000.00 in six equal install-
ments of $500.00 each, one in-
stallment to[9] be paid on the last
working day of each month during the stated period of employment. The party of the[10] first
part also covenants and agrees
to pay the said party of the second part a commission on net
sales[11] in like monthly pay-

ments based on records examined on the 25th of the month during which the commission[12] was earned.

In Witness Whereof, the parties to this Contract have hereunto set their hands and seals, the day and year[13] first above written. (263)

333▶ Mr. Frank S. Ferris, 262 Green Avenue, Tarrytown, New York 10591.

Dear Mr. Ferris: I see no reason to point out at any great length the respects in which I disagree with[1] the contentions made by you in your January 26 letter. I should like to say, however, that I have[2] interviewed my client at length and I know that a defense of estoppel cannot be made out in this case. One reason[3] for this is the lack of knowledge on the part of our client of certain of your client's activities, which[4] knowledge I suspect you are wrongfully assuming our client had.

With respect to the differentiations[5] between our respective clients' magazines made by you in your January 28 letter, I think you[6] will agree that there are cases on both sides of the question dealing with the significance of such differentiations.[7] You are no doubt aware of those cases that say that there can be changes in the future in format,[8] logotype, and design.

I cannot agree with your characterization of our client's magazine title[9] as "highly generic." The Patent Office did not consider it so. I am sure that you will agree that a[10] generic name as opposed to a descriptive name, on the other hand, can be registered where it has acquired[11] the necessary distinctiveness. Very truly yours, (230)

LESSON 73

334▶ APARTMENT LEASE

THIS LEASE, Made this first day of October, 1966, by and between Harold Meyer, of the City of[1] St. Louis, Missouri, hereinafter called lessor, and Mayfair Corporation, hereinafter called lessee.

WITNESSETH:[2] That said lessor hereby leases to said lessee the following portion of the building No. 1800[3] Kingshighway Boulevard in St. Louis, Missouri, Apartment 15H, on the 15th floor, east side,[4] for a term of two years, beginning October 1, 1966, and ending September 30, 1968,[5] and the said lessee agrees to pay for the use and rent thereof a total of $3,600.00,[6] payable at the rate of $150.00 a month, for the whole time and to pay the same on[7] the first day of each month, in advance, at the office of the Mayfair Corporation.

The lessee covenants and agrees[8] with the lessor as follows:

1. To take good care of the premises and keep them in good repair, free from filth,[9] danger of fire, or any nuisance, and return the same, at the termination of the lease, in as good condition[10] as received by him, usual wear and use excepted.

2. To not sublet without the

written consent of[11] the lessor.

3. To make no alteration in the premises without the consent of the lessor in writing,[12] except ordinary repairs as aforesaid.

4. To use the premises only as a private residence[13] and not display signs or advertisements on the premises or keep anything on the outer window[14] sills; to keep the entrances and halls free from obstructions; and not to do or permit to be done any other[15] thing that will annoy, embarrass, inconvenience, or injure the lessor or other tenants in said building.

It[16] is further agreed that the lessor will:

5. Furnish hot and cold water and heat in season during the term of[17] this lease, unless prevented by circumstances beyond his control.

6. Keep the halls and entrances clean and in[18] good repair.

The lessor or his agent shall not be liable for any damage or injury to the[19] lessee, his servants, or his guests occasioned by water, snow, or ice or by neglect of the janitor, other[20] tenants, or occupants of adjacent property.

At the expiration of the term hereby created, or[21] if default be made in the payment of rent after the same is due, or upon the breach of any of the[22] covenants and agreements herein contained, the lessor or his agent shall have the right to enter and take possession[23] of the leased premises, and the lessee agrees to deliver same without process of law.

IN WITNESS WHEREOF,[24] the parties have hereunto set their hands this first day of October, A. D., 1966, to duplicate copies.[25] (500)

335▸ PROXY

PROXY Solicited on behalf of the management for the annual meeting of stockholders to be held[1] April 21, 1966, in the Grand Ballroom of the Beverly Hilton Hotel, Santa Monica[2] and Wilshire Boulevards, Beverly Hills, California.

The undersigned hereby appoints Wilson Adams and[3] James Ashby, and each of them, attorneys, agents, and proxies of the undersigned with full power of substitution[4] to vote all stock of the undersigned in Adams Foods, Inc., with all the powers the undersigned[5] would possess if personally present, at the annual meeting of its stockholders to be held on April[6] 21, 1966, and at any adjournments thereof, upon the election of directors for[7] the ensuing year, upon the resolutions concerning indemnification of directors and officers[8] against litigation expenses in certain circumstances, and upon ratification of the[9] directors' appointment of Haskins and Sells as auditors. (190)

336▸ POWER OF ATTORNEY

KNOW ALL MEN BY THESE PRESENTS

That I, Perry Clark, of the City of Roselle Park, Union County, State of New Jersey,[1] have made, constituted, and appointed, and by these presents do make, constitute, and appoint my wife, Mary[2] Helen Clark, my true and lawful attorney for me and in my name, place, and stead, to act as my agent in the[3] management of my property, real and personal, of whatsoever nature and wheresoever situated,[4] giving and granting unto my said attorney full power and authority to do and perform all[5] and every act and thing whatsoever requisite and necessary to be done in and about the premises,[6] as fully, to all intents and purposes, as I might or could do if personally present, with full[7] power of substitution and revocation, hereby ratifying and confirming all that my said attorney[8] or her substitute shall lawfully do or cause to be done by virtue of these presents so long as I shall[9] be outside the territorial limits of the United States.

IN WITNESS WHEREOF, I have hereunto set[10] my hand and seal the 21st day of December, A. D., 1965 (214)

337▶ Mr. Bryon S. Mead, 87 Chimney Road, Stamford, Connecticut 06902.

Dear Mr. Mead: On March 20, 1966, Joseph Finlay suffered serious personal injuries[1] and property damage of a permanent nature solely as the result of the negligent operation[2] of a motor vehicle by your insured, Frank W. Holt, of Winchester, Massachusetts. Mr. Finlay was a[3] passenger in Mr. Holt's car at the time of the accident.

It is my understanding that you are the Nationwide[4] Insurance representative in charge of the file relating to this claim against Mr. Holt. Therefore, you[5] are the proper person to discuss the possible settlement of this claim.

I have suggested an immediate[6] suit, but Mr. Finlay recommended that you be given an opportunity to discuss the matter[7] first. Very truly yours, (144)

LESSON 74

339▶ Mr. Louis C. Fletcher, Publisher, Direction Magazine, 29 Chandler Drive, New York, New York 10007.

Dear Mr. Fletcher: We are attorneys for Shaw-William Associates and the officers of that company.[1]

Our attention has been called to an article entitled "Businessman's Ethics," which appears in the February[2] issue of Direction. In our opinion, the article libels Shaw-William Associates.

Recognizing[3] the integrity and responsibility of Direction, our clients and we are surprised that you would[4] publish so important an article, involving such complicated issues and mentioning Shaw-William so[5] conspicuously, without at least contacting its officers to verify the facts.

This article grossly[6] distorts what has actually transpired and reports inaccurately and unfairly the judicial and[7] administrative proceedings relating to this important matter.

In view of these matters, we hereby request[8] that a retraction of the libelous and defamatory statements in the article be published immediately.[9] Sincerely yours, (183)

340▸ OPENING STATEMENT

In this case, the evidence introduced by the plaintiffs will show that these various plaintiffs and their neighbors have[1] resided in the neighborhood in the vicinity of 33 Bradley Street for a great many years; that[2] the neighborhood developed as a residential neighborhood; that it is now and has been for many years[3] occupied as a residential neighborhood, including many homes that have been developed as comfortable[4] and enjoyable places of residence.

That it was a quiet, undisturbed, and delightful neighborhood; that[5] within about a year or within less than a year, the business of quarrying and stone crushing was introduced;[6] that the ledge from which the stone is taken is a very large ledge; and that the continuance of this industry[7] means that the plaintiffs and their neighbors will be subjected to a nuisance that will continue for perhaps a[8] generation.

In the conduct of this business, a process involving the blasting out of a ledge, large holes 6 inches[9] in diameter or thereabouts are drilled from the top of the ledge to a depth of from approximately 40[10] to 80 feet and are charged with a large quantity of explosives. As a result, sections of the side of[11] the ledge are blown out. And those pieces of rock resulting from blasting in turn have to be

again blasted by small[12] blasts.

That these pieces of rock, when reduced to sufficiently small size, are transferred to a stone crusher and there ground[13] into smaller sizes and more or less uniform sizes. The business thus carried on includes a large electric[14] motor, large stone-crushing machinery, a large derrick, a steam shovel, drop ball and air drills, drop drills, and other[15] machinery.

As a result of the operation of this business, there is a tremendous noise resulting[16] from the electric motor, the stone-crushing machinery, the operation of the derrick, the operation[17] of the steam shovel, the operation of the air drills, the operation of motor trucks and other[18] machinery, and blasting. This noise is made up of rumbling, heavy noise; shrieking whistles; the pounding noise resulting[19] from the electric motor; the loud, tapping noise resulting from the air drills; and the sharp noise resulting from[20] the blasting. In attempting to describe these noises, I do not pretend to give a fitting description. The witnesses[21] themselves will describe the situation with regard to the noise in their own way. (436)

LESSON 75

342▸ Williams & Andrews, Attorneys at Law, The First National Bank Building, Danville, Indiana 46122.

Gentlemen: Re: Standard Products Company v. Nelson. Our client in the above-entitled action does not deny that he was partly responsible[1] for the collision between his passenger car and your client's truck, but the fact that your client's driver did not[2] signal for a stop shows contributory negligence on his part.

It is our opinion that the court will not[3] allow you the full amount of damages named in the complaint, even if you should win the case. In view of the[4] circumstances of this accident, we are willing to settle at this time with a payment of $250,[5] an amount sufficient to cover the actual damage to the company's truck.

In making this[6] offer, it is not to be construed that we acknowledge a major responsibility for the accident[7] upon our client. Our purpose is to save our client from litigation and the time-consuming expense of[8] litigation. Sincerely yours, (164)

343▶ POWER OF ATTORNEY

KNOW ALL MEN BY THESE PRESENTS: That I, Glenn Bosley, of the city of Beverly, county of Essex, state of[1] Massachusetts, have made, constituted, and appointed, and by these presents do make and constitute and appoint Susan[2] Farrelly, my secretary, of the city of Beverly, county of Essex, state of Massachusetts, true and[3] lawful attorney, for me and in my name, place, and stead, to act for me in connection with my business as[4] president of the New-Way Calculator Company in Beverly:

1. To draw checks against my account in the[5] Citizens Trust and Savings Bank.

2. To endorse notes, checks, drafts, or bills of exchange that may require my endorsement[6] for deposit as cash or for collection in said bank.

3. To accept all drafts or bills of exchange that may be[7] drawn upon me, giving and granting unto my said attorney full power and authority to do and perform[8] all and every act and thing whatsoever requisite and necessary to be done in and about[9] the premises, as fully to all intents and purposes as I might or could do, if personally present,[10] with full power of substitution and revocation; hereby ratifying and confirming all that my said[11] attorney or her substitute shall lawfully do, or cause to be done, by virtue hereof. IN WITNESS WHEREOF,[12] I have hereunto set my hand, this tenth day of October in the year 1966. Signed and acknowledged[13] in the presence of us. (265)

* * *

▶ If you have to make a correction after you have removed transcribed material from your typewriter, place the original on a clean sheet of paper and erase your mistake. When you put the copy back into the machine, set the typewriter for stencil to type in the correct characters. If the copy is in the right position, you can proceed to type as usual.

Unit 16

LESSON 76

344▶ To: Mark C. Lambert, President, From: Manager, International Sales, Subject: Advertising in Clipper Cargo Horizons.

Enclosed in a copy of Pan American's Clipper Cargo Horizons. This monthly publication, designed[1] to promote worldwide marketing, is printed in six languages and distributed to almost 200,000[2] business executives on six continents.

You will notice that keyed advertisements from several different[3] countries seek suppliers of electronic components. In order to see the kind of inquiries we get,[4] I answered all these advertisements in the current issue. These advertisements may provide the contacts we want[5] with foreign distributors, especially those in Thailand and West Africa.

It might be a good idea[6] for us to insert a keyed advertisement ourselves to try to attract the type of distributor we want. Let[7] us wait, however, until we test the response to my inquiries before attempting this approach.

Just as soon[8] as the responses to my inquiries have been tabulated and analyzed, I will send you my report.[9] (180)

345▶ Mr. Wilbur R. Adams, Peninsular Hotel, Hong Kong, British Crown Colony.

Dear Mr. Adams: You have been authorized to purchase 1,000 bolts of raw silk for use in our dress factory.[1] However, we want to caution you to obtain a comprehensive certificate of origin for all[2] goods purchased in the British Crown Colony. It is impossible to clear these goods for U. S. customs[3] without this certificate from the Hong Kong Government. It must state that the merchandise covered is not considered[4] to be of Chinese or North Korean origin within the meaning of the Foreign Assets Control[5] Regulations of the Treasury as agreed upon by the governments of Hong Kong and the United States.

We[6] do not think that you will have a great deal of difficulty in obtaining raw silk that meets the requirements of[7] the certificate of origin; however, we have heard of a number of companies that have been disappointed[8] when they tried to import brocaded silk, which usually originates in China. More difficulty[9] is experienced in trying to clear customs with goods purchased in the New Territories than with merchandise[10] from Kowloon or Hong Kong Island.

We had complaints about the quality of the last raw silk we obtained in[11] Hong Kong. It was not as firm as the material we usually buy, and dresses made from it pull at the[12] seams. Please watch this factor and try to buy silk that does not "give," even if it means paying a slightly higher price[13] than we suggested. If you find that you cannot get the quality we need, you may want to wait until you get[14] to New Delhi to purchase the silk. From our standpoint, though, we prefer the faster delivery that we get from[15] Hong Kong. Sincerely yours, (304)

346▶ Air France, 683 Fifth Avenue, New York, New York 10019.

Gentlemen: In confirmation of our telephone conversation, I should like you to reserve a conference room[1] at Orly Airport for eight of our executives on July 11 from 11 a.m. to 5 p.m.[2] (Paris time).

Mr. Harold Nicks and I will arrive on Flight 82 at 9:30 and continue on[3] to Frankfurt that evening at 7:30 on Flight 63. Two representatives from our Paris office[4] will attend.

Please make flight arrangements for the four executives listed below and notify them of their[5] schedules at the addresses listed on this letterhead:

Edwin E. Walker—Wiesbaden
Ralph L. Sparks—Oslo
Marvin[6] C. Atkins—Brussels
Howard G. Botsford—London

Please bill Bestway Motors here in Baltimore for their transportation[7] and arrangement expenses. Mr. Nicks and I have already arranged for our tickets.

I am depending[8] on you to handle these important details so that we can have as successful a conference as we had[9] last year. Sincerely yours, (184)

* * *

▶ A portfolio with one or more pockets to hold small notes, cards, and memos will be of great help to you in keeping your material organized when you go in to take dictation. An inexpensive file folder to which you have attached several paper clips can substitute for the portfolio.

LESSON 77

347▶ To: Millard D. Weston, Vice-President for International Trade, From: Manager, International Sales, Subject: Restrictions on Imported Components.

As you know, we have been using our Veracruz factory primarily for the assembly of construction[1] equipment from components imported from the United States.

In an effort to force foreign manufacturers[2] to use a growing percentage of locally produced components, the new Industry and Commerce Secretary[3] intends to extend the policies already enforced against the automobile industry. In that[4] area the government requires that 60 percent of the finished product be of Mexican origin.[5] United States businessmen have been told to expect that the list of industries required to use Mexican[6] components will next be extended to include those manufacturing diesel engines and construction equipment.[7]

I recommend that we curtail our Mexican operation by 25 percent immediately and[8] that we watch for political clues before we make our next move. (171)

348▶ Mr. Arnold G. Thompson, Administrative Assistant, Mod-

ern Office Equipment, Baltimore, Maryland 21204.

Dear Arnold: On Thursday morning the Administrative Committee approved your proposal to spend three weeks in[1] Europe to make a preliminary investigation of sites for our new calculator plant.

We think that[2] you should go first to Brussels, because it is so generally regarded as the business capital. It[3] is the home of the Common Market or European Economic Community (France, Italy, West[4] Germany, Belgium, Luxembourg, and the Netherlands). The European Coal and Steel Community and Euratom[5] (the agency for coordinating development of peaceful uses of atomic power) are also[6] located there. These three agencies comprise the new Administrative City.

As you might suspect, foreign[7] subsidiaries abound in close proximity to these headquarters. There are more than 500 of them, including[8] 150 American branch offices. You will want to request an appointment with an[9] EEC Official Spokesman's Group specialist in office equipment, even though he will probably give little[10] help to a company that may provide competition. One of the American law firms in Brussels might be[11] much more helpful in suggesting leads for plant location. You will get some help, too, from our Chase National Bank[12] representative. I also have several business contacts to whom I will give you an introduction.

After[13] visiting the Common Market countries, you may want to investigate opportunities in the Outer Seven,[14] known as the European Free Trade Association (EFTA), for a possible site. Included[15] are Austria, Britain, Denmark, Norway, Portugal, Sweden, and Switzerland.

Although we suggest that you start your[16] investigation in Brussels, you will have to proceed from there on your own initiative. After you have completed[17] your itinerary, please present your plans to John Smathers and me. Sincerely yours, (356)

349▶ To: William P. Shea, President, From: Manager, International Sales, Subject: Purchase of Multi-Jewel Watch Company.

I recommend that Time Control investigate the desirability of purchasing the assembly plant[1] of the Multi-Jewel Watch Company in St. Thomas, Virgin Islands.

In an effort to stimulate the economic[2] growth of the Virgin Islands, the United States has never charged a tariff higher than 6 percent[3] on any of their imports; however, importers of foreign-made watches must pay 50 percent duty. The[4] advantage given to the Virgin Islands has caused a whole new American-owned watch assembly industry[5] to develop there.

A company based in the Virgin Islands can produce a 17-jewel movement for[6] $3, much less than the labor costs in the continental United States. Since

1959, eleven[7] subsidiaries of United States-owned watch manufacturers or importers have invested $5,000,000[8] in plants in the Virgin Islands. Production has leaped from 5,000 units in 1959[9] to more than 2,400,000 units in 1964. In fact, today twice as many watches[10] are produced in the Virgin Islands than in plants in the United States. Our producers have discovered that[11] they make greater profits by manufacturing abroad and importing foreign watch movements from the Virgin Islands[12] than by confining production to the United States.

In my opinion, we should join the trend. (258)

350▶ Aruba Trading Company, Nassaustraat 7, Oranjestad, Aruba, Netherlands Antilles.

Gentlemen: We have shipped you today the cameras listed on the enclosed Invoice No. 18742[1] via the Royal Netherlands Steamship Line freighter "Ammon." Since this ship calls only at Curacao, it will[2] arrive six days after leaving New York.

Our Quickomatic camera retails in the United States for[3] $67.50, and we had hoped that you could sell it at that price in Aruba so that it could[4] compete favorably with Japanese and German cameras also sold there. However, we cannot offer[5] you the additional 15 percent discount that you requested so that you can maintain the standard price in[6] the United States.

We realize that you cannot

sell the Quickomatic to American tourists at a[7] price higher than they would pay at home. However, we feel that it will compete very favorably with cameras[8] manufactured in other countries among tourists other than Americans. Cordially yours, (178)

LESSON 78

351▶ Mr. Charles M. Goodson, Manager, Union Rubber Company, 12-2-16 Higashi-cho, Teramachi-Gashira, Kimikyo-ku, Tokyo, Japan.

Dear Chuck: I was glad to hear that your flight was a good one and that you are getting established in your new home. I[1] am sure you will enjoy your home away from home in Tokyo.

Here are a few additional pointers on foreign[2] credit:

1. Rely heavily on National City Bank's Tokyo branch for credit information. Although[3] we have an account with the Nippon Bank, we have found that foreign banks are very conservative and will seldom[4] reveal financial data about their clients. Use the Nippon Bank for double-checking, but regard National[5] City as your primary source of credit information.

2. Always check the latest U. S. Department[6] of Commerce WORLD TRADE DIRECTORY for type of organization, sales territory, size of business, sales[7] volume, trade and financial reputation, and trade references.

3. Follow up all trade references submitted[8] by the Japa-

nese buyer. In addition, of course, the home office will be working with the international[9] division of Dun and Bradstreet and with the Foreign Credit Interchange Bureau of the National[10] Association of Credit Men.

Because of Japanese government restrictions on conversion of yen into[11] dollars, you must accept payment in foreign currency, which can be used for plant expansion; however, you should[12] be in constant touch with our bank about the desirability of hedging against unfavorable currency[13] exchange by selling yen for future delivery. Your banker can give you details on how future delivery[14] contracts can protect us against unfavorable market changes.

Until you are thoroughly adjusted[15] to business methods in your new locale, please check with me very carefully on all credit matters. The[16] success of our operation depends largely on our establishing good credit relations with dependable[17] buyers.

Give Marge my best. Sincerely yours, (349)

352▶ To: All Members of the Administrative Committee, From: Manager, International Sales, Subject: Steel Importation.

At the weekly sales and production meeting next Thursday, May 22, we shall discuss the desirability[1] of importing steel for use in our Omaha factory. Our purchasing agent has been asked to prepare[2] and distribute pertinent cost data prior to the meeting.

In addition, here are some figures from last week's[3] meeting of the National Industrial Conference Board that you should have at your disposal for this meeting:[4]

Imports this year will hit between 7 million and 8 million tons, compared with last year's record 6.4[5] million tons. Probably the increase is attributable to strike hedging.

Some imported steel products undersell[6] their domestic equivalents by as much as $50 a ton. Steel bars from Japan, for instance, are[7] delivered in Los Angeles at $53.32 a ton less than the domestic price.[8] Cold-rolled and hot-rolled sheets from the same sources to the same destination are $26.20 and[9] $33.50 less per ton, respectively.

Domestic steel companies are increasing their plant-expansion[10] budgets. With automated equipment they will probably compete more successfully with foreign[11] producers both in quality and price, but this doesn't help the present situation.

The fact remains, the steel[12] industry has not regained a favorable balance of trade that was lost seven years ago. The severe strain on[13] the American economy induced by this unfavorable balance of trade may induce the Administration[14] to curtail imports. Thus, any decision we may make to import steel should be implemented immediately.[15] (300)

353▶ Aruba Trading Company,

Nassaustraat 7, Oranjestad, Aruba, Netherlands Antilles.

Gentlemen: Thank you for telling us about your experience with the Quickomatic. We are delighted that[1] it competes favorably with cameras from Germany and Japan.

Naturally, your large reorder pleases[2] us. It is being shipped today from New York aboard the Royal Netherlands Steamship Company's freighter "Isis."[3] Our Invoice No. 18998 covering the shipment is enclosed. Please deposit the amount due,[4] $433.14, to our account in the Holland Bank.

We have followed your suggestion[5] about printing operating instructions in Dutch, Spanish, and French. We have not included these instructions in[6] the boxes containing the cameras, but we are sending you a supply in each language so that you can give[7] the customer the translation he requests. Cordially yours, (150)

LESSON 79

355▶ Diamond Office Equipment, Box 893, Geneva 6 Eaux-Vives.

Gentlemen: We wonder whether there would be any objection on your part to having our forwarders in New[1] Orleans pay the inland freight on our orders coming from your American factories. We have this arrangement[2] with several of our other suppliers, and it works very well. Actually, we think that handling it[3] in that manner would mean less work for you;

it would have several advantages for us, too.

Under the present[4] system we receive your bills for transportation after we receive the bills for the principal value. Sometimes[5] this delays our cost calculations and pricing. Also, the bills for transportation sometimes do not specify[6] complete information about the number of machines covered or the invoice number.

I am enclosing copies[7] of 15 recent invoices having inconsistencies in carrying charges and weights. I have marked them[8] to illustrate my point. The errors on them, however, average out; therefore, we think it wise not to attempt[9] to adjust any previous charges. If in the future, though, you will send the machines on a freight-collect basis,[10] we can work out any discrepancies with the carrier.

Please let us know whether this arrangement will be[11] satisfactory. Yours very truly, (224)

356▶ First Merchants Bank, 8 Boylston Street, Boston, Massachusetts 02116.

Gentlemen: We are enclosing our letter of credit for $295.63[1] in payment of your customer's documentary sight draft against the Vargas Import-Export Company of[2] Kingston, Jamaica.

This amount is in payment of Invoice No. 67023 of the Ideal Lighting[3] Company for flashlights and acetylene lamps. Sincerely yours, (71)

357▶ Diamond Office Equipment, Box 893, Geneva 6 Eaux-Vives, Attention of Mr. Michael

Jones, Export Administration Supervisor.

Gentlemen: Thank you for your letter of April 7 about our last order. In due course we did receive your letter[1] of November 22, but the thought never occurred to us that you were withholding shipment until we[2] paid for the goods. You have been shipping on open account for the past five years and sending us invoices after[3] the shipments were made.

To obtain the permission from our Exchange Control Board to buy dollars for payment of this[4] order, we shall need your invoice. Please send it in quintuplicate by return airmail; you should have our remittance[5] about ten days after we receive the invoice. Yours very truly, (112)

LESSON 80

Dictated Letter

358▶ Dear John:

Yes, we do have a program under way at the Kansas City plant about which we are enthusiastic. We feel it is very effective; possibly it would apply to your operation. This is the way it works:

At their regular foremen's meetings, the superintendent selects a department to be inspected. No one else knows beforehand which department it will be. The group spends a short time, perhaps fifteen to twenty minues, in the department; and each man writes down suggestions. The inspection is not confined to safety exclusively but covers safety hazards, housekeeping, production methods, equipment, waste, etc. The recommendations are consolidated, typed, and distributed for discussion at the next meeting.

The people concerned feel the program has been effective in maintaining housekeeping, in correcting defects, and in numerous other ways. The major benefits arise from the efforts of the foremen themselves to be ready, rather than from the specific suggestions. Cordially yours,

P.S. There are six filmstrips in that series entitled "Supervisory Problems in the Plant"; and they may be purchased singly, in pairs, or in a complete set. We have used them to good advantage.

359▶ Suggested Form for Report

RULES FOR PAY FOR TIME NOT WORKED

I. APPLICATION OF RULES

Only those payments that are specifically covered in this manual shall be made for time not worked for any reason.

For the purpose of applying these rules, the number of hours in a working day, a working week, and a working month has been defined as follows:

One working day	8.0 hours
One working week	40.0 hours
One working month	173.3 hours

These definitions do not constitute a schedule of working hours, as the actual working hours of field personnel may vary considerably from one day to another.

If in any instance the application of these definitions should not be appropriate to the circumstances, the facts in the case shall be presented to the vice-president concerned for review and decision.

II. ABSENCE

The provisions of this section refer to the effect of absence on payments of salary and on payments of cost of living bonus, where applicable. For special rules covering the effect of absence on semiannual bonus payments, see pages 15 through 19, Paragraph IX.

A. Company Business

Time spent away from regular work because of company business shall not be considered time absent.

No deduction shall be made from the salary of an individual who is away from regular work because of company business.

B. Holidays

See page 9, Paragraph VI.

C. Illness or Injury

Individuals absent because of nonoccupational illness or injury shall receive a percentage of their salary based on their length of service, providing the absence is approved by the district manager in the case of representatives, or by the vice-president concerned in the case of individuals on or above the district manager level of responsibility. For rules covering payments in the event of occupational accident or disease, see page 10, Paragraph VII.

If the individual returns to work but subsequently suffers another period of illness from the same or related cause, his eligibility for future salary payments shall be determined in the following manner:

1. If the individual returned to active employment for a period of three months or longer, the second period of illness shall

be regarded as a new illness and salary payments shall be handled accordingly.

2. If the individual returned to active employment for a period of fewer than three months, the second period of illness shall be regarded as a continuation of the first and salary payments shall be made accordingly, beginning the first day of the second period of absence. If the individual received the maximum allowable salary under the schedule above during the first absence, no further salary payments shall be made.

If an individual returns to work but subsequently suffers another period of illness from a different or unrelated cause, the second period of illness shall be regarded as a new illness and salary payments shall be handled accordingly.

D. Jury Duty

An individual receiving a subpoena for jury duty would be paid the difference between the sum received for such service and regular salary for the hours absent because of jury duty.

E. Marriage

An individual absent to get married shall be paid for the regular hours absent up to and including five regular working days, provided a leave of absence has been previously obtained from the department head. The five days' pay shall not be granted if a leave of absence of more than one calendar week (excluding paid vacations and paid holidays) was taken for this purpose.

F. Leaves of Absence Without Pay

The amount by which the salary of a monthly payroll employee shall be reduced in case of absence for which pay is not allowed shall be computed by dividing the salary for the month in which the absence occurred by 173.3 hours. The resulting amount shall be deducted for each working hour for which pay is not allowed.

Suggested Telegram

360▶ Mr. Eugene Carletti, Thomas Baker and Company, 713 North 22 Street, Sacramento, California.

I am leaving for South America on May 10. Urgent. Telephone me before then; otherwise, send to my secretary immediately data you were compiling for me. E. R. Harper

361▶ Suggested Form for Memorandum

TO: David T. McGrath   **FROM:** E. R. Harper

DEPT: Personnel   **DEPT:** Personnel

SUBJECT: Bonus Plan Participation   **DATE:** June 4, 1966

In accordance with standard procedures, the qualifications of the individuals listed below have been reviewed; and it is recommended that they be approved 100 percent bonus participation effective July 1, 1966.

Employee	Job Title	Employment Date
Charles Bond	Salesman	January 13, 1960
Anne Marie Clarke	Secretary (Mgr.-Marketing)	June 3, 1958
Elizabeth Ann Eller	Secretary (District Mgr.)	October 15, 1953
James T. Fischerman	Salesman	April 21, 1960
S. J. Jabowitz	Salesman	May 5, 1960
Faye Keaner	Secretary (Controller)	April 8, 1957
L. B. Kruse	Salesman	February 20, 1960
Arthur Paine	Salesman	June 16, 1960
Sam Petersen	Salesman	May 16, 1960
Joan Lee Seaton	Secretary (District Mgr.)	March 18, 1959

Will you please place consideration of these recommendations on the agenda for the next meeting of the Salary Committee.

cc: Mr. Hopkins

RECALL DRILLS

▶ **Joined Word Endings**

1 Treatment, alignment, supplement, amusement, compliment.
2 Nation, termination, station, connotation; credential, confidential, essential, social, initialed.
3 Greatly, namely, nicely, nearly, mainly, clearly, tightly.
4 Readily, speedily, easily, hastily, steadily, family, necessarily, heartily.
5 Careful, thoughtful, delightfully, mouthful, helpfulness, dreadful, useful.
6 Assume, assumption, resume, resumption, presume, presumption, consumer.
7 Dependable, profitable, reliable, laudable, gambler, cabled, payable.

8 Gather, gathered, together, rather, either, leather, bother, bothered.

9 Yourself, myself, itself, himself, herself, themselves, ourselves, yourselves.

▸ **Disjoined Word Endings**

10 Neighborhood, childhood, motherhood, brotherhood; backward, forward, upward, rewarded.

11 Relationship, steamship, editorship, membership, professorship, championship, worship.

12 Radical, technically, political, critical, chemical, article.

13 Tabulate, congratulate, congratulation, regulate, regulates, regulated.

14 Willingly, exceedingly, knowingly, surprisingly, grudgingly, smilingly, longingly.

15 Readings, mornings, sidings, dressings, drawings, sayings, blessings.

16 Program, programmed, telegram, cablegrams, diagram, radiogram.

17 Notification, modification, specifications, gratification, classifications, codification, ratification.

18 Personality, ability, reliability; faculty, penalty, casualty.

19 Authority, seniority, majority, minority, clarity, sincerity, sorority.

▸ **Joined Word Beginnings**

20 Employ, empower, embarrass; impress, impression, implicate, impossible.

21 Increase, intend; encounter, enforced, encourage; unwritten, unkind, unsuccessful.

22 Refer, resign, receive, reform, repay, reorder, reorganize, react.

23 Delay, deliver, depart, debate, deserve, diligent, digest, digit.

24 Dismiss, discover, disappoint, disclaim, discuss, despite, desperate.

25 Mistake, misquote, misspell, misstate, misunderstanding, mishap.

26 Comprise, comfort, comply, compress; condition, consult, continue, confident.

27 Submit, submerge, substantiate, subdivide, sublease, sublet, suburban.

28 Almost, also, already, altogether, alter, alteration, alternative, alternate.

▸ **Disjoined Word Beginnings**

29 Interested, internal, interview, intercept, introduce, introduction, enterprise, entrance.

30 Electricity, electrician, electrical, electric wire, electric fan, electric iron.

31 Postman, postal, postage, postmaster, postdate, postpone, postponed, postcard.

32 Supervise, supervision, supervisor, superhuman, supernatural, superlative, superimpose.

33 Selfish, self-made, self-defense, self-respect, self-conscious; circumstance, circumstances, circumstantial.

34 Translate, translation, transform, transmit, transatlantic, transit, transportation.

$9x$ $93 \div 4 = 5 \times 35$